Why Black Women Are Alone

Why Black Women Are Alone

✦

The Truth Revealed

Henry E Bullard

iUniverse, Inc.
New York Bloomington

Why Black Women Are Alone
The Truth Revealed

iUniverse books may be ordered through booksellers or by contacting:

iUniverse
1663 Liberty Drive
Bloomington, IN 47403
www.iuniverse.com
1-800-Authors (1-800-288-4677)

Because of the dynamic nature of the Internet, any Web addresses or links contained in this book may have changed since publication and may no longer be valid.

The information, ideas, and suggestions in this book are not intended as a substitute for professional advice. Before following any suggestions contained in this book, you should consult your personal physician or mental health professional. Neither the author nor the publisher shall be liable or responsible for any loss or damage allegedly arising as a consequence of your use or application of any information or suggestions in this book.

ISBN: 978-0-595-51653-7 (pbk)
ISBN: 978-0-595-61981-8 (ebk)

Printed in the United States of America

iUniverse rev. date: 4/29/2010

Contents

Introduction

This book is to explain from a male's point of view as to why so many black women are struggling to keep a man. They can get a man no problem, but keeping one, that's a whole different subject. In this book you will hear the **COLD, RAW,** and **BRUTALLY HONEST** truth about black women that has for so many years been considered taboo, or the elephant in the room that no one will talk about and has been diluted in the comedy routines of black(and some white) comedians. We will uncover why black men date outside their own race (white, Asian, mail orders brides etc.) and discuss the **real** reasons (not the politically correct ones) for this behavior.

Women for many years (**especially black women**) have put out countless books, magazines and made movies about how men are no good and always pointing out the many flaws and mistakes we have. Books and movies like **"Waiting to Exhale"** and while the movie was directed by a man its source originated from a woman. But what about these scandalous two timing black broads? I want every guy reading this book to think throughout their entire life from childhood to now; who were the most **rebellious**, most **sneaky**, most **secretive, two faced** people growing up? Was it the boys? Or the girls? Who were the ones sneaking out of their bedrooms to meet **'old boy'** down the street that their parents **TOLD** them to stay away from?! Every guy reading this book knows exactly where the hell we're coming from. (Bullard) "One of the dumbest, most ridiculous, naive statements I've ever heard was and I quote: *"There's no such thing as a no good woman. Every no good woman was made no good by a no good man!"* Now I don't know if a black man, or black woman made that statement, or even if they we're black period! I will however be the first one to say that is by far the most **ignorant**, most **foolish**, most **uneducated**, statement I've ever heard anyone make in my short life!!! To say a statement like that is to say that women are perfect, and do absolutely **no wrong**, and we all know that's a **LIE FROM THE PIT OF HELL!!!!** Women do **more** dirt, tell **more** lies, and have **more** secrets than **any** man will ever have! Especially **BLACK** women!"

This book also represents for the **GOOD** black men out there that get taken advantage of all the time by these two timing black women. These are good black men that really do love and care about the women in their lives, but these black women have always taken advantage of that. They either use them for their money and resources, or they keep them as platonic friends while they run around town with the guy that they **know** is gonna dog them out! Many **good** black men are frustrated, tired and confused by black women's behavior. How they're always saying they want a good man, but when they get one they either dog him out or find some reason why they don't like him (We'll get into their many excuses later in the book). (Bullard) "One of the inspirations for writing this was Tariq "K-Flex" Nasheed's book "The Art Of Mackin" a friend of mine came up to me one day when I got off work and told me about this book. At first I wasn't interested, I had never even heard of the guy. But after some thought, I went a local book store and read some of the material, and I have to say I was **very** impressed at how logical and truthful I found it to be. And when I stopped to think about it, every type of female he named, I knew or still know to this day! **I even dated some of these women!** But as true as it was, I also said to myself *"Why the hell does it take all this to be with a black woman?!* I also noticed how a lot of women were turned off by the book and how they didn't want to read it, and they **REALLY** didn't want their men/husbands to read it!"

We've noticed that when it comes to situations where women are being called out on **their** problems and issues all of a sudden they don't want to hear it and they get real defensive and angry when the truth is spoken. A perfect example: Chris Rock's movie "I Think I Love My Wife" that man was sexually frustrated because basically his wife wouldn't "put out" anymore. And she had no **logical** explanation as to why she didn't want to have sex with him. And when he was tempted by another woman, he gave in to the temptation (Or he almost did anyway.) She had the **audacity** to get angry with him! Every man who saw that movie knows that he would have been completely justified if he slept with that woman! And you know what? Every **woman** knows it too! That's why they didn't want to go see it, and they didn't want their men or husbands to go see it either!

Readers of this book we are not doctors, nor are we specialist of any kind. We are not therapist, or do we claim be any type of relationship experts. We're just two regular everyday guys who have been through serious problems and experiences with black women. We've also seen and witnessed close friends and family members go through the same things. But, maybe it should be the regular guys who speak on this subject. No doctors, no therapist and their intellectual rhetoric, or some psychologist trying to analyze every single word or action you do. With all due respect to these people we mentioned, we're more about telling it like it is and not necessarily trying to find some **deep, philosophical, and psychological** reason as to why black men and women act this way. Not everything is **"deep", "philosophical", and "psychological!!!"** Some things you just have to be practical about and just use **common sense!!!** Many black women who read this book will say that we are arrogant, or we don't know what the hell we are talking about. A lot of women will be very angry, so angry in fact that they won't be able to finish this book. But they're gonna have the nerve to want to have a discussion about it! They're gonna say this book *"pissed them off"*, and they know that it's *"not referring to them"*. But let us also remind you, why do we assume that the black women, who are saying these things, are good black women to begin with? **Because they say they are?!** Often times it is the guilty who speak for themselves and put themselves on blast before anyone can bring up a railing accusation against them; you just got to give them enough rope to hang themselves with.

A lot of women will say we're "bitter" and "angry", while we don't know about the bitter part we certainly won't deny that we **are** angry. We are **very** angry! Angry at the fact a lot of **good** black men take the rap or get the shaft by a lot of black women who are bitter and vindictive! Black women who know what they're doing when they manipulate, lie and use these good men to get what they want! Even the so called **"good black women"** are guilty of this to some degree! Whether they are **"consciously"** or **"unconsciously"** doing it, it's being done by them too! (You'll see how in the "Friend Factor" chapter) A lot of women will also try to hide this book from their man or husband saying *"You don't need to read this book it ain't talking about nothing!"*, but if it ain't talking about nothing, why the hell are they trying so hard to stop you from reading it? Or they cop an attitude when they see you reading it, and say *"if you read that book we're through!!"* We assure you black men **RUN** and find a spot to read this book if they're saying that! We can assure you that at one point in your lives, you have known or **know** black women like this (Some of you are even married to them, but that may change after you read this!!). **Please keep in mind this book is not pertaining to all black women JUST SOME!!!**

There are some black women out there who take care of their business, and do what needs to be done, and don't take their man or husband for granted. If you're this woman then this book **doesn't refer to you**, so please don't be offended by this! But if you are this type of black woman, keep reading there are some things you need to hear and it will hurt **A LOT!!!** (The truth tends to do that!!!) But just deal with it, because this has been a long time coming for you, and you know it! Also we are not by any means putting, white women, Asian women, etc. on any type of pedestal either. This book is not just for black men as well. Any man of any race will find what we have to say **very** interesting. Any man from any race can use this as a reference to weed out "bullshit" women, regardless of their race. A lot men from other races are venturing over to black women, and while that is completely your business, we as black men have a duty to tell you what the hell some of you are getting into!!

We also know automatically black women are gonna point the finger at the other race of women and point out their flaws. They'll say *"White women, Asian women, etc. do the same things we do!"* But do you notice that the one's that are guilty of this, are always the one's quick to point the finger?!! It goes all the way back to the garden of Eden, when Eve ate the fruit and God asked her *"What is this you have done?"* and Eve replied *"The serpent deceived me and I ate it"* You see? Eve was guilty of wrong doing and when God called her out on it, **immediately** and **automatically** she pointed the finger at someone else!! (Eve was a black woman by the way.) We didn't say that white women, Asian women etc. **didn't** act this way!!!! There are white women, Asian women, etc. who are just as corrupt and scandalous as black women, but there scandal and flawed ways **pale** in comparison to a black woman's scandal and corruption! We are speaking in general terms about **all** the races in this book. We know there are **exceptions** to the rules of everything we discussed, and we know you black women will try to exploit that in every single way just to absolve yourselves! But, to all you black women out there who are always shouting for honesty, well here it is! The **cold, hard, raw, honest**, truth as to why you are **alone!**.... Fair warning: **THIS IS GONNA BE DARK AND VERY VERY UGLY!!!!!**

1

The Problem

In this first chapter "The Problem" we will go over the basic problems most black women have. Most black are alone today mainly because of their attitude, from day one black women are raised to be highly opinionated and always speak their mind no matter what! There's nothing anybody can tell them, everything has to be their way, they don't respect men at all, and the ones they **do** respect are the ones that treat them the worst. They disrespect one another all the time and call each other "bitches and ho's" but as soon as you (black men) call them anything, all hell breaks loose! Black women want everything but are not willing to give the best of themselves to get it. What we mean for example: Black women want the **best** of everything, but are not willing to give the **best** of themselves to get it!

They want the most expensive dinners, the best rides, the biggest houses, and the most glorious life imaginable but only want to put in half the work. (We will dive deeper into the _"why"_ in the later chapters of this book) You could take a black woman to a top notch restaurant, pick her up in the flyest whip, treat her every way you're suppose to treat a woman, and still at the end of the date if she feels like it she'll "think about" giving you some? Well in that case we could've ordered a call girl from an escort service, done the exact same thing and at least gotten what we wanted out of it sexually. Now we know most of you black women are up in arms right about now, ready to hit something (or someone knowing you all!) but let us remind you, it's the **mentality** we're trying to get at. Most black women know off top what the hell they're doing before they get started on any date anyway, mostly because they've already scoped him out and assessed what they're going get out of it, and what little they're going to put in to it. Then when you take them out they try to put the man on a guilt or defensive trip by saying little comments like _"Well I just don't get down on the first night"_, or _"I hate it when men take women nice places and then expect them to give them some at the end"_. Automatically we will get defensive or have a small guilt attack because there's that first impression thing. *"I don't want to get lumped in the same category as those other Men"* or *"Man, she must be a good girl who's tired of men always wanting some from her"*. **Game!!!** My brothers all of it is game!!! Don't buy into that shit for one more minute!

Most of the time all they want is money anyway, but the "trippy" part is they don't want to work to get it. That includes you independent women too! (Black men don't be fooled or thrown off guard for one minute because she's an independent woman with her own job and own money that she's not a gold digger. Most of them have this *"Better your cheese than mine"* attitude so keep your game tight fellas!) They want nothing less than the perfect man who is: perfect body, perfect face, and most importantly perfect bank account, and someone who will put up with their crap!

Work too much for too little.

Another problem with black women is you have to work way too hard to even get with them! Black women feel like you owe them something just for even talking to them. They put on this stuck up act turning down men all day, and then go home alone and holler *"Men ain't shit!!!"* Black women have a list of **"*must meet*"** qualities that benefit them and only them. It's never *"What can I do for him"* it's *"What can he do for me?"* *"How can he make my life better?"* *"What can I get out of him?"* But as we said earlier the first thing you got to have is money, no matter how you get it, you just better have it! Without it, it's a done deal. Another quality they require men to have is that you have to be willing to give them **what** they want, **when** they want it, and they don't care if they hardly know you or not. Ask any man that's ever been to a club, a black woman and sometimes more than one will walk up to a complete stranger and ask him to buy her and/or their friends a drink. Then you have the audacity to be offended or upset when we follow you around, or ask you for some. **Listen!!!** We black men work way too hard for the money we make, and if you got the gall to ask us for a drink and you barely even know us **or even like us**, then we got just as much **"balls"** to ask a woman who has asked us to spend our hard earned money on her, for some ass, or at least 20 minutes of her time!

A lot of black women pretend to like men so they can get a drink out of them, but as soon as they buy it they want to disregard them and blow them off. Then they wonder why he clicks on them and goes upside their head. Well we don't blame any of them one damn bit!!! **Buy your own damn drinks** and we won't have this problem or just decline when we offer. Let us get this straight, we're good enough to buy you a drink, but not good enough to sit down and talk to? (Bullard) "My dad always used to say to my sister" *"If you don't like a man or you're not interested in him don't accept anything from him, no matter how bad you want it or need it!"* When a man offers you something, drinks, money, to pay a bill etc, if you're not interested in him don't accept it! When you accept anything from us, we think you have accepted **us** in general! We know what a lot of you black women are saying right now *"Well I just got to get this bill paid, or I really needed to get this done, it was important!"* Ok, then, when he comes around looking for something in return (and you know what we mean!) and you turn him down, watch him go all ballistic and talk about what he bought or what he did. Anything from, paying a phone bill, to buying an ashtray for your coffee table in your living room, believe me he's going to blow up!

Ungratefulness

A black woman will let you go down on them with no intentions on returning the favor, and if they do, they have an attitude about it. That, to us makes you a selfish person. Don't get us wrong, black women have some good qualities, but at the end of the day it just ain't worth the hassle. A lot of black men can feel us on this. Fellas you've tried to get that ass, done everything you can possibly think of and when she **finally** decides to give it to you, you're like *"Damn, is this it?!"* That little half-ass lazy blow job or weak dick riding she does is all you get, and then she has the nerve to sit there and look at you like you're supposed to be satisfied or something. **Give us break!** Did we half-ass when we did the things we did for you? Even the sexual things?

Another problem black women have is that you run off at the mouth talking about things you know nothing about, like telling a man how to be a man. Have you ever been a man? Do you know what we go through just to put up with, and deal with your sorry asses? There's just no satisfying you! If we bought you a Cadillac, you'd want a Bentley! If we bought you a tennis bracelet you'd want a diamond ring! If we bought you a house on the hills, you'd want **a house by the lake!** Nothing we ever do is good enough for you, and you wonder why so many black men are dying at a young age because of heart attacks or depression, or some are just up and leaving. Well we would leave too! We wouldn't want to be somewhere, where we are not appreciated! Then we got these black women yelling *"I don't need a man to raise my baby!"* True, you could raise a child without a man, but that doesn't mean it's to be done! You could walk through a floor of broken glass barefoot if you **had** to, but that doesn't make it a good idea!

Sexual Stinginess

Black women don't feel it's a priority to please their man. A black woman will do something freaky **ONE TIME** and never do it again, or she'll put you through **HELL** before she does it again! (You have to wait, or she only saves it for special occasions like your birthday, or an anniversary, or when **she's** in the mood.) Listen! If you are not into something sexually, do us black men a favor and don't ever do it!! When you do certain freaky things he's going to want that as part of his sexual routine. And foolish black woman, why wouldn't you want to keep doing that if it turns him on and keeps him in the house?! Contrary to popular belief it's not that hard to keep a man. We only require the basics.

1.) Food (A woman that can cook)

2.) Silence (Don't talk so much. Know when to be quiet.)

3.) Sex (You got to freak your man to keep your man.)

But here's the thing. It's got to be the type sex that we want and like. Don't just give us any type of sex and expect us to be satisfied. True he's not going to turn down sex if you offer it to him because he is still a man, but don't try to ration out the "twat" to what **you** think he deserves! To all you black woman that do that, you have only yourselves to blame when he cheats! Then you sit there crying talking about *"I can't believe my man cheated with some other girl who was giving him oral sex for an hour and a half."* or *"would have a threesome with another woman".* That's right black women, the **ONE** thing you don't do, or refuse to do could mean the difference between him cheating or staying! Black men don't feel bad for leaving or, wanting to leave because your woman or wife wants to "hold out"; who the hell does she think she is anyway?!

Independent Bitches

We have talked a lot about the problems of black women and their many faults. But now we are going to get into probably the worst of the lot, the so called "Independent woman". These women by far are the worst out of the whole group of black women we described in this whole chapter. First of all they don't want a man unless he has as much as they have or more. You hardly ever see a successful black woman with an everyday average working Joe. Then even if they get a regular guy, they will hold their success over their heads. Most successful black women are unapproachable anyway, it's like as soon as you come up in the world all of a sudden you have this long list of requirements that a man has to have before he can even think about approaching you!

People say all the time *"Hey, don't be afraid or intimidated to walk up to these independent sisters"* That's just some bullshit excuse women use **(ESPECIALLY BLACK WOMEN!!!)** to make themselves feel better and to cope with their loneliness! It's not that we're afraid or even intimidated; it's because they won't **SUBMIT** or do what the hell their told or even **ASKED!!** They have forgotten a woman's place!! And while their out there playing the role of a man, and trying to emasculate every man that tries to even step to them, you're just digging yourselves into a deeper and deeper grave of solitude by your own stupid pride!! **(We hope you black female celeberties and six and seven figure a year broads heard this, especially you female rappers!!! You broads REALLY have a tendency to act like guys!!!)** It's not that we're scared, it's just that **IT AIN'T WORTH THE HASSLE!!!!** It's not worth the looks and stares we get when we even try to approach them! They have this set of standards that is virtually **impossible** to meet, and even if we did meet it, as we said earlier you wouldn't be satisfied anyway! Dating a successful black woman is like filling out a job application! No matter what profession they are, from doctors to lawyers, to high profile businesswomen, to CEO's of large corporations, to even black female celebrities it's the same story everywhere you go. We're not saying all of them are like this but **some** of them are, and they know it! (Bullard) "Every brother reading this book can feel me on this. There's nothing more aggravating, more obnoxious, no one more **stuck up** and difficult to deal with then a black woman that **"DONE CAME UP"!!!!** Give that broad a desk with a "supervisor" title on it, or an "executive" position and all of a sudden they're **"Queen Sheba"!!!** *"Can't no man do nothing for* *me!!"* **SHUT UP!!!!** And humble yourself!!!! That's why you're **dumbasses** ain't got you nobody now, because *"Can't no man do nothing for you!!!"* So they just **don't!!!"** They always want to be treated as equals but as soon as it's time to accept the consequences of a man, then they want to be treated like women. This goes out to all black men (and men period) in society, if these black women want to step up to you like a man start treating them like one! These women want to nag and argue if things aren't going the way they want. They will do anything to push your buttons, some will even go as far as to hit you, but as soon as you hit them back now all of sudden you're the bad guy! Well then, so be it fellas! At one point you got to take a stand, and if it makes you look like the bad guy then that's a burden you'll have to bear!

2

The "If" Factor

Now in the last chapter we talked about the many problems that some black women have. In this chapter and in the other's to come we're going to deal with specific flaws and set backs. And one of the things that we noticed about black women is everything is always conditional when it comes to them, we call it the **"If"** factor. We've asked so many black women so many scenarios like _"Would you go down on your man for an extended length of time?"_ and she answered _"Yes, if he were paying this bill."_ Why is it that everything comes at a price for black women? A black woman will do special favors, or **sexual** favors for a man, boyfriend, or even husband, but only if her conditions are met. We asked another black woman _"Would you ever get up and go to your man's house at 5:00 in morning to cook him breakfast, even though you didn't have to be at work until 9:00a.m.?"_ And she replied _"Yeah, if he were paying my bills, and if he were my man for a long time, and if he had a lot of money, and if"...._ Blah, blah, blah!!!! The list went on and on, if he did this, if he did that, **if, if, if, if.**

Wake up black women!!! That's a turn off!!! No man wants to feel like he has to pay for love, favors, attention, or even sexual experiences. Like we said in the last chapter if that's the case we may as well find a prostitute, or a call girl of some sort and pay for it! At least it will be the type of sex that we want, because it will be no different than what you're asking us to do. We realize some of the examples we gave were somewhat extreme (but true), but these are problems that many black men get from their women or wives everyday. And the point is not the favors it's the **mentality** were getting at! This is why more black men are paying for sex, and going to strip clubs, and finding all types of brothels to hang out at, because what you're asking is no different really than what their asking! And, at least if we do it this way, we won't have to go through all these conditions, and red tape, and hoping we'll get some, and if we do get it, get it the way we want it!!!

We've heard black women say so many times *"Girl, men always want you to do something freaky to them like "Suck my dick" or "Give me some, then I'll pay your bill"*. And our reply is, **you damn right!!!!** Since we're in the business of negotiating, you came at us with a condition we're going to come at you with one! This is how we have the bartering system, *"I'll give you this, for this"*. That's not how a relationship is supposed to work! You'll find that if you did things out of the shear kindness of your heart and stop always putting a condition on everything, you would get a whole lot further with men than you think! Men notice little qualities like that and pick up on it right away, and he will not hesitate to do something for you too (if he's good man that is.) Don't get us wrong, we're not saying that you shouldn't have some standards, or some boundaries, but all this if, if, if, crap has got to end! And true, there are some men out there who will take advantage of that type of kindness, and if that's the case then ladies get rid of him immediately! We're just trying to get you to understand the mentality you have. If you do something, do it because you want to, or because you get a kick out of seeing your man's reaction and stop worrying about *"What am I getting out of it"*. If you go that extra mile for him, believe me he will notice, and go out of his way for you too.

A lot of black women right now have their noses up in the air, and their just a twitching and itching with anger saying *"Who the hell do these guys think they are?!"*, but let us assure you that the one's that's feeling that itch and squeamish feeling in the pit of their heart or stomach are the one's that act this way because you know we've touched a nerve. **Deal with it!!** Get a drink of water, sit up straight and **deal with it!!** Because we're just getting started! A black woman who is secure and mature in herself, won't get offended by this because, she knows she's handling her business, and even if she's not, she will take this as constructive criticism and apply it to make themselves a better woman for their men, or their husbands. We realize this wasn't a long chapter but it was an important issue we needed to point out, so that black women could grasp the concept of how "screwed" up their mentality is! Trust us the next chapters will get pretty lengthy so get comfortable as you get ready to read it.

3

The Masochistic Mind

In the first chapter we discussed the various problems of black women, and in chapter 2 their conditional ways of love. Now we're about to get to the meat of the subject. But, before we do that though, let's look up the technical meaning of the word "*Masochistic*". The American Heritage Dictionary of the English Language describes *masochism* as: 1. *Psychiatry. An abnormal condition in which sexual excitement and satisfaction depend largely on being subjected to abuse or physical pain, whether by one's self or another. 2. A. The deriving of pleasure from being offended, dominated, or mistreated in someway. B. The tendency to seek such mistreatment. 3. The turning of destructive tendencies inward or upon one's self.* Now we could end this chapter right now seeing that we just basically described just about every black woman in America, however we will go deeper.

It seems the worse you treat a black woman, the more she likes it and wants you. Many black women can't handle a good man no matter how much they say they want one! (Bullard) *"I'm sure a lot of people want 300 million dollars, but that doesn't mean that every one can handle it!"* One, of the **many** ignorant statements that we've heard black woman give as a reason for not getting with a good guy is *"The reason I don't like him is cause he's too nice!"* How the hell can a guy be too nice?! What sense does that make?! That's the exact type of twisted logic we would expect to come from a black woman, you say you want a good man and then when you get one you turn him away because he's too nice? We have even witnessed men talk bad to black woman, we mean just dog them out, and they just stand there, smiling and giggling and constantly coming back for more! This guy told us how his step brother got into an argument with this black woman, after the argument was over he drove past her house shooting at it numerous times. Did you know this girl called him later that night talking about how much she loved him and wanted to do all this different type of sexual stuff to him? (Bullard) "I mean the two of us are sitting there just flabbergasted, I mean it just blew our minds!"

We have male friends that tell us how they have dogged black women out, called them all kinds of names, and just completely disrespected them, and yet the woman is just as sweet as she can be toward them. They're saying how they're just going to do this and that for them. Take them here and there, and buy them this and that. And we're thinking, *"What the hell is their problem?"* *"He doesn't like you, he doesn't respect you, and treats you like crap, yet you still keep coming back to his ass!"* *"Or you'll go find someone else who's just like him or worse!"* Why do you do this to yourselves? And then you black women have the **nerve;** we mean they have the straight up **audacity** to ask God for a good man! We're pretty sure God is in heaven saying ***"You stupid black woman, I've sent you 10 good men and what did you do with them?!!!"***

Then, on the other hand we've seen guys (and we've experienced this ourselves!) treat black women with the utmost respect, talk to them like they're actual "human beings" and be perfect gentlemen to them. And we have heard (and experienced) them making statements like *"I don't know what it is about him, I just don't like him"* or *"Girl, he's boring"*. Black women don't even know how to act when a good man is approaching them or addressing them. We have seen in the clubs and other places; black women respond quicker to *"Bitch come here!"* as opposed to *"Hey, how are you doing? My name is etc."* and that's a damn shame! *"Nice"* simply means *"weak"* in the eyes and mind of a black woman plain and simple! On that same note a majority of black women say they want a thug or a criminal. Have any of you black women looked in a dictionary lately? Do you know what the definition of a thug or criminal is? And this is what you want for a man? Then you sit there and wonder why you have a bad relationship and can't understand why this is happening. Even in entertainment, black women sing songs, write books, and shoot videos all basically with the same content. They're all dating some thug or ex-convict, or they're singing about how they want a thug or a "Hood Boy" in their life. There is an old story that goes: There was this woman who came upon an injured rattle snake. After looking at and feeling sorry for it she decided to nurse the snake back to health. Overtime she had come to care about the snake, and one day when it had completely healed, she went to pick it up and the snake bit her on the cheek. And, as she lay there dying she asked the snake: *"Why?"* and the rattlesnake replied: *"You crazy bitch you knew I was a snake!"*

Black women know what they're getting into when they meet these guys. It's not like they're stupid or something, they know trouble when they see it! They know what he's about what he's been doing; they see all the red flags from a distance. And, yet you **still** want to walk into these troublesome relationships anyway, why? Well we can tell you why, for most black women the main part of it is sex. We've heard black women say so many times when they've told us or their girlfriends about the problems they were having with their boyfriends or husbands, but when we or they asked them *"Why don't you just leave him alone?"* they would always reply *"**Cause girl you just don't know, ooooohhhh!!!**"* Is good sex really worth it, at the cost of piece of mind? It's like having money without being truly happy. Sure, it will feel good for a minute, but without the peace to go with it, it will only provide a temporary fix and you'll soon begin to yearn for something more. So why do you keep him around? Well, we'll tell you why, because contrary to popular belief, **black women think with their clits, just as much as black men think with their dicks!** Don't let them tell you any different! They would rather have a guy that's "**fucking them good**", than a guy that's "**treating them right**"!

If you don't believe it black women, look at the men you've dated or been with, or are in a current relationship with now and evaluate everything else besides the sex. Then see what else he's contributing to the relationship and your life for that matter. Another one of the most ignorant statements we've had the displeasure to hear come out of a black woman's mouth is *"I'm not trying to teach no nigga nothing! Either you know how to please me or you don't!"* Well, how the hell is he supposed to know, if you don't **tell him** or **teach him?** Like we said, black women would rather have a man that's **fucking them good**, than a man that's **treating them right!** Most of you are too ignorant and too selfish to realize that sex is a **skill** and not a **talent!** By that we mean it's something that can be learned and not something you're necessarily born with. Did any of you black women stop to think; that if you took that good man and taught him how to please you the right way that you would have the total package? That can be done, but you cannot take a trifling man who's screwing you good, and teach him responsibility, character, how to go out and get a job (and keep one!) and pay the bills on time, you can't teach a man how to be a man! You're not raising kids here, you're in an adult relationship, and if he doesn't have it together already he ain't gonna have it together **and you can't make it happen!!!!** The saddest part about all of this is if you black women look back in your life long enough, you had some good men that really did love you and care about you. But no!!! You wanted a thug or a "Hood boy" because you thought it was **"exciting"** at the time!!! No wonder we have no respect for you, we good black men that is! We can't really respect someone who doesn't have any respect for themselves, and since that's the kind of guy you always want and always take back into your life, what's that say about you?!!!

A Theory by Hank Bullard

"I'm sure a lot of you heard of the 80-20 rule. A recent Tyler Perry movie "Why Did I Get Married" kind of made the saying and phrase popular, but it's actually a saying that has been around for a very long time. It's a saying that goes. "In a relationship people are always gonna be 80 percent of what you want", and that is true. But, my issue is why do black women **intentionally** go after the 20 percent? As we said earlier a black woman would rather have a man that's fucking them good, than a man that's treating them right! In Tariq "K-Flex" Nasheed's book "The Art of Mackin" he bought up an **EXTREMELY** good point about being **"Sexually Undisciplined"** and how one can let their sexual appetite over take them and they can't control their "urges". Most black women are guilty of this. They let the **"urge"** and the fact that they **"GOT TO HAVE IT"** cloud their good judgement and common sense! And, while you're just going after the 20 percent which is dick, you leave the 80 percent like we said, responsibility, character, getting and holding a good job by the way side! We also said that black women say things like *"I ain't trying to teach no nigga"*, but, I say if you took that man with the 80 percent and taught him the 20 percent you liked, you would have 100 percent of a man, right? But, because your lack of desire to communicate with him (which is nothing but laziness when you really think about it!) you toss him aside! Often times God will leave us as an incomplete project or task just to make us communicate with each other! **THE FUN IS IN LEARNING BLACK WOMEN!!!** You ask God to send you a good man and he will, but you're going to have to do some work to maintain the relationship as well! God made the earth, but that didn't stop Adam and Eve from having to maintain it! God loves you, but that doesn't mean he will absolve you of **human responsibility!** There is some level of work you will just have to put in ladies, and there's no way around it! While I agree with most of Tariq's book, I personally believe that black women are **waaay** more **"Sexually Undisciplined"** then men!! They just know how to **"play the game"** better so they don't come off looking like a ho!!!!"

Then there's the other type of black woman, the kind that fall for these men with issues. These irresponsible, problem having, always got drama type of men that they always have to baby and mama all the time! You can't handle a good man either because you're so used to having problems and issues in your relationships. When that good man comes along with no problems and no issues and does have his shit together you can't handle it, because you're so used to being in control, and coming to his rescue, and straightening everything out for him. And when you finally meet a man who doesn't have these issues he's *"boring"* and *"I can't figure out why I don't like him."* So you gravitate back to that same type of man you had before because, **you are hooked on drama!!!! And pain!!!!! And problems!!!! And issues!!!!** And that has become your *"normal"* and what we good black men can't figure out is why?!!

An experience told by Jaquiez Douglas

"Most of my views come from my personal experiences with black and white women. I have dealt with both races on many occasions. I once dated a black woman and I had really strong feelings for her. When, I first met her she already had a boyfriend and she dumped him on the spot to be with me (that there should have been my first red flag). She claimed she loved me and only me. For months, I played the role of the faithful boyfriend and, I thought, I had a faithful woman. I bought her gifts, was there for her when she needed me, I even kept money in her pocket. One day I called to talk to her, and she was very stand-offish on the phone. She tried to get me off the phone as I tried to talk to her and, finally I told her I'd call her back. But, before I said goodbye, I told her *"I love you"*. She hesitated, and said *"ok"* and hung up the phone. I called her back and reminded her that she didn't say *"I love you too"*. Her response; *"Uh, my boyfriend's over here"*. **What kind of shit is that?!!** Come to find out this black bitch has been seeing this guy just a long as she had been seeing me! She's been sleeping at his place, she's been fucking him, and all the money she was getting from me, she was giving to this guy so he could get his car fixed. When it all came down to it, she gave this guy a total of $5700 dollars of my money, and then she left me for this guy. I moved on and so did she, but this same dude she left me for and was so loyal to started cheating on her. He started taking her money, and stealing from her. When she had finally had enough and felt she was going to voice her opinion on the matter, he started beating on her **(severely!!!)**. She finally left after he went out of town one day, but some months later she called me and told me what had happened to her, she was trying to run back to me (ha ha!!) but I wasn't having it!"

This story was a classic case of the typical black woman we mentioned throughout this chapter. They get in these situations **THEN** you want to remember who was good to you and who was there for you, (guess an ass whooping will do that to you!) But the thing is why the hell does it take all that before you come to your senses? We will explain why in the next chapter in a minute but his story is a lot like many other good brothers done wrong by no good ass black women. No matter how bad he treated her she stayed more loyal to him than Jaquiez, and constantly pushed him to the side and disregarded him. It wasn't until the situation got almost life threatening that she came to her senses (and in most cases a lot of black women don't even come to their senses then!) Why do you black women do this to yourselves? Why do you love those that hate you, and hate those that love you?

4

The Friend Factor

In this chapter we will go deeper into the masochistic mind by looking at the men black women don't date.... **The good ones!** For years we've seen and experienced all the time how black women will constantly run back to the arms of these no good, trifling, lowdown men or thugs, and always look the good man in their life over. Believe it or not there are some good, stable, got it together, men already in black women's lives. But those are the guys that black women keep as *"friends"*. They say shit like *"Oh he's just a good friend"* or *"He's like a brother to me"* or *"I just don't like him like that!"* or some other lame ass excuse why they can't get with them.

They always want to come and spill their heart out about what their man or husband did to them while the friend is supposed to sit there and just listen and give advice while hiding his feelings from her. And, here is the twist, for our good black men out there, and we hoping you're listening real good to this, most black women (or women period in this case!) **already KNOW or have always KNOWN how you have felt about them!** Women are not stupid in the least, but we've seen and experienced so many black women used this fact to serve there own selfish purposes and desires. To be that shoulder to cry on, or to get a male opinion about something or someone. Naturally, the good black man has a nice heart so he keeps a certain degree of hope (and sometimes naively so, we admit!) that she will see the light, but guys she never will. She will just continue to use your feelings and manipulate them as we just said for her own selfish reasons and purposes, because she wants the best of both worlds. Black men **enough!!!!** You are worth more than that, you are better than this!! **She's using you!!!!** Whether she is doing it consciously or unconsciously, leave her alone!!! Let her go be with her trifling ass man, and see if she cares one damn bit if you step out of her life! Because, truth be told she's probably got two or three other guys just like you anyway. As long as she has her *"fucking friend"* she could care less if you walk away or not.

To all you good black men out there, don't be apart of some black woman's **"team"**. They all got'em, there's the **"fucking friend"** who we said earlier is usually treating them the worst. There's the *"confidant"*, the good guy in her life that she's always complaining to, and pouring her heart out with. He has all the qualities that she wants and looks for in a man, but she's too much of an **idiot**, or too much of a **selfish, greedy ass bitch** or, **all the above** to realize it! Then there's your other type of distant friends, your *"rent man"* your *"watch the kids man"* your *"get something to eat man!!"* He's the guy she calls when she wants a free meal. She calls him, because she knows he likes her and will "Mack" a free meal out of it. But, we tell you kick them all to the curve.(Bullard) "This is what I was refering to in my theory in the "Masochistic Mind". Black women know how to get what they need from each guy so they don't come off looking like a ho or slut!! And they know how to make you feel guilty by giving the other "friends" some bullshit sob story as to why they're not ready to give up the goods! *"I don't wanna ruin what we have!"* or *"I'm going through some things!"* and *"I just got out of a relationship and I need time to sort things out!"* She knows that the good or nice guy has a good heart, so excuses like this are gonna invoke sympathy or inspire some kind of guilt trip. But catch her at her place at 2 or three 3 o'clock in the morining and see if she's not getting **THE BOTTOM KNOCKED OUT OF HER ASS** by some lowlife you haven't seen or heard of! That's right! All the platonic friends know about each other, because she talks about each of them to each other. But, I guarantee you, **ALL** of you "platonic friends" there's **ONE** friend you all don't know about!!" So Unless you're the *"fucking friend"* tell her that you and her have nothing else to discuss. If she wants something or asks you to do something for her, **dismiss her immediately!** Tell her to *"call that nigga you fuckin' to go do it for you!"*

Retired and Prudish

Another problem black women have is when they do finally decide to settle down and get with the good guy they want to calm their whole persona and demeanor. They have done all that buck wild shit with the other guy and now they want to bring their tired, worn out asses to you in hopes of settling down. All these years you've had to hear about all the freaky buck wild things she's done with all these so called "wrong guys" and now that she's with you, or married to you now, all of a sudden *"I'm not into that anymore"* is what she tells you. Or even worse she doesn't like to have sex as much with you as she did with the other guys! She was fucking like a jack rabbit in heat when she was with the so called *"wrong guys"*, but now that she has gotten to you, now she's like *"I don't be wanting to do it, as much as I used to!"* Let us ask you a question black women, if you're not into doing all that freaky buck wild stuff now, or fucking like crazy when you get to us, what the hell makes you think **we** want you now?!!! We're no different than the guys you dated when it comes to what we want sexually, and the wild things we're in to as well, the only difference is, had you stayed with us you wouldn't have had half the drama you had when you were dating "ol boy". Now, this man is frustrated and pissed off because he feels he's been cheated, on what seemed to be the best and most exciting part of her life, and he feels bad because now when he tries to get her to do some of those things and she won't do them, he gets mad and asks *"why?"* and she'll give a bullshit answer like *"I don't do that kind of stuff now"* or the **ultimate lame ass excuse of all time:** *"I just don't see myself doing stuff like that with you."* What kind of bullshit answer is that?!! What the hell do you think attracted us to you in the first place? And now you want to sit there tell us something like that? Let us ask you black women something, how do think that makes us feel inside? If anything, the good one is the one that deserves it! How would you like it if something like that was said to you by someone you loved and cared about?

An experience told by Hank Bullard

There was this woman who I used to date. We had known each other for 20 plus years of each others lives, our families even knew each other and we had grew up together right down the street from each other. We had always been close and have always had a special bond and connection with each other. I had known many other women in my life as long as I've known her, but we didn't connect like this. We had gone together a few times when we were teenagers but it didn't work out, but we still remained close friends and that bond was still there.

When she was going through a bad time in a relationship and needed someone to talk to, not minding, I became that person. Since we had gone together twice when we were teenagers there was still kind of a spark there, and as I consoled her more and more, that spark began to grow and grow. We were always seeing each other whenever we could, and had gotten to the point where we couldn't wait to be around each other. Eventually we ended up falling for each other (hard too, or at least I did anyway!) It was a feeling and a romantic connection I had never felt before in my life, and mind you, I had been in love before on a few different occasions so I wasn't new to the feeling. But this was different, this was on another level, because we had already known each other for so long and already knew each others likes and dislikes. There was really no *"getting to know each other"* because we already did, and that's what made the connection so cool in the first place.

To make a long story short she was still dealing with her current relationship and me at the same time (That was my **first** mistake) and, as that part of her life began to clear up she began to drift away further and further. As weeks and weeks went passed she just kept drifting even further from me emotionally and romantically. As she got further from this guy, and I guess *"getting back to normal"* (If that's what you want to call it) She, kept constantly stressing how good of "friends" we were and just that. She started hanging out with the same type of guys she usually dated again and started to avoid me all together. But, this woman would still have the nerve to call me like were still just *"good friends"* and call to tell me about her problems with this person, and that person, and this guy and that guy, like I'm one of her **"homeboys"** or **"girlfriends"** and, I'm thinking to myself *"Damn, do you know who the hell you're talking too?"* How **tactless** was that? To talk about another guy to another guy, especially if it was a guy that you were once romantically involved with. It was as if that time we had didn't even exist at all, and she had forgotten completely about it. Like the fool I was (I admit it.) I hung around for a while, hoping that if we went out enough times, or if I kept telling her how I felt that she would have a change of heart, but to no avail that day never came. Eventually, it all led to one big argument and I finally asked the question *"What are you saying? That you're not in love with me anymore?"* and her reply was *"You don't really want me to answer that do you?"* which basically meant no. Keep in mind this was only a few short weeks after, so if she fell out of love that quickly then that means she was never in love to begin with in the first place. And like I said, like a fool, I tried to get this woman back, being her friend, listening to her problems, helping her in any way that I could.

Until one night, she was at my apartment, and I was trying to get close to her, but she kept rejecting me. When she finally left, it all hit me like a ton of bricks. *"She's not gonna be with me"* I thought. *"She never was"*. And, in that one eye opening moment I had to come to a startling reality *"I was the rebound guy!"* I said to myself. All this time, I was somebody she just leaned on for emotional support, and while she got the best of me, I was never on her agenda period. I was just her "string along guy" that she could talk to, while she ran wild with these other guys, not even taking into consideration once how it made me feel!! So I told her finally over the phone that I didn't want to speak to her anymore, and, I didn't want to be bothered with her either. And, do you know what her reaction was? (Not to my surprise). This nonchalant, cavalier attitude, like I was just telling her any old news or something. *"Well I guess I'll talk to you later then"* was all she had to say to me. And I'm like *"wow"* I thought to myself, *"After all this time, that's all you have to say?"* It was if she just shrugged her shoulders and said *"Eh, oh well'*, and just kept going about her business. You know what was really worse than any of that? It's wasn't the fact that we didn't get together or become a couple, although that's what everybody thinks because I'm sure that's what she told everyone, that she wouldn't be my "girlfriend" so I cut her out of my life. But, I can assure you readers of this book, I am not and have never been that immature or that **petty!!** I would never cut a woman out of my life just because we didn't *"get together"!* We had gone together twice and had broken up, but still remained friends so **that** was never the issue! The part about all of this that got to me, was after all these years of knowing each other friendship wise and romantically, she never even **TRIED** to give me another chance with her. She never made any attempt to even **TRY** to regain those feelings that she had once had for me. After everything that had happened, as long as I had known her, she couldn't have at least given me **that much**?! She tossed me aside as if I were nothing. Whether she did it consciously or unconsciously that's what she did!!! She made me feel like everything that ever happened in our 20 plus year relationship was a joke, and **that's why I cut her off!!!!!"**

It's a sad thing what happened between the two of them, but even worse than that was her whole reaction to it. Like we said earlier fellas, if you cut them off, they could careless because they've gotten what they needed from you anyway and will find someone else (if they haven't already) to replace you and leave you picking up the pieces. She was a **USER**, plain and simple! Whether she was aware she was doing it or not that's what she is, and that's what she was doing! (Bullard) *"She could care less"* I thought to myself. It's not like she put up much resistance when I told her I was through with her, in fact she didn't put up **any resistance at all!** *"Well I guess I'll talk to you some other time then"* was all she had to say, and just like that, it was over, and she didn't, and doesn't even think twice about it to this day". "Did you know months later she still had the nerve to call and try to talk to me about some other guy she met a few months earlier? *"I don't believe this!"* I thought to myself. *She's never gonna change, she never will."* When I called her out on it, all she could say was *"I'm sorry"* but what good did that do? Sometimes *"I'M SORRY"* **JUST DOSEN'T CUT IT!!!!!!!!"** Don't be **sorry!!!** Think about what you're doing and saying!!!"

See what we mean guys, and (black) gals? Hank, was just her leaning post till the crisis was over, as soon as it was, it was back to the *"friends"* category for him. Do you all know that, this woman **(Like most women that think like this)** still has the nerve to believe that she hasn't done anything wrong to this day? **(Like most black women think)** Completely oblivious to the fact that a great relationship was lost, and she doesn't even see it **(or care)**! Do you even know that this woman called sometime later and did the exact same thing all over again?! She called again like everything was just "okay" with them, like nothing happened! She asked if he had a girlfriend or was dating anybody, and she guessed because he answered the question, she felt that gave her the "green light" to ramble the fuck on about all the guys she was dating and had been talking to! And, the only reason Hank didn't **"cuss her ass out"**, was because quite frankly, he just didn't care about her anymore! Any other woman with any type of **sense** would know that that is **disrespectful** and it is **tactless** to do that!

We heard this comedian one time telling a joke he said "Ladies, you have a male friend in your life that likes you, and you know it, stop treating him like that. It's like going to a job interview and the owner saying *"This is a good resume! You got all the qualifications…. but sorry we're not gonna hire you. Yeah, we'll probably hire someone with a drinking problem and who's constantly late. But, is it okay if we call you from time to time to complain about the guy we hired?"* That is so much like black women it's scary! We're the applicant's, and they're the bosses hiring. They see this great resume, but still won't give us the job, but wanna complain about this *"loser"* they hired to us. You black women say men aren't shit, but you have a male friend that pretty much fits the description of everything you want, and yet you keep him as a "friend"? What's wrong with this picture? Are you dumb? Are you blind? Are you stupid, simple or slow, or all of the above? Black men, this is your wake up call! She's never gonna come around, you're just wasting your time. She's running game and playing with your head!

Sub Chapter-The Safety Net Guy

As we explained earlier in this chapter black women use the good guy that they know likes them and/or is in love with them for their own selfish purposes, in this sub chapter we will explain why. If it's one thing a woman needs in her life its security, and basically that's what the "friend" is for. He's the *"safety net guy"* or the *"fall back guy"* or what a prestigiously well known comedian said in one of his routines *"A dick in a glass case"*. Black women have no intention of getting with the good guy, but they show them just enough attention to keep them holding on. You're her "insurance", her "parachute pushover" if the bottom falls out of everything you're the guy she calls to get that loving or attention she didn't get from her hoodlum, or weak ass man.

Another Experience by Jaquiez Douglas

"I once dealt with a black woman who was with a no good ass man. The guy cheated on her, degraded her, and just completely disrespected her at any given moment. I liked her, and treated her like a queen, but she would always say that I was everything a woman could want, but she never wanted to be with me. I was just her shoulder to cry on; she would remain faithful to this jerk, but would keep me on the back burner. He would dog her out and she would call me as her safety net, so I got tired of it and cut her loose. Do you know this broad got the nerve to get mad at me? Are you serious?!!!" There is a joke that is very old, and it goes: *Every black woman has the mentality that they want 4 animals. They want a mink in their closet, a jaguar in their garage, a tiger in their bedroom and a jackass to pay for it all"*! Although it's been told humorously in a lot of comedy routines, it is the absolute truth!! That's exactly what black women want, they want a guy to be this thug ass bad boy they can have fun and cut loose with, do all these wild and freaky things with. Then they want a "good guy" to play the therapist role, to console them, fill in that empty void in their lives that the bad boy is not filling. The only problem is it's the good guy that's getting screwed over! As soon as she's all better its back to the back burner for him and back to the abuse for her, as Jaquiez said in his story. The funny thing about a safety net is when you remove it, all of a sudden the whole game changes! Like Jaquiez said in his story when he finally got sick of it, and told her to *"piss off"* she got a serious attitude!

That's right!!! Fellas, if you ever just told her about herself, or just got rid of her all together, you will see how she truly felt. Like Hank said in his story, you will notice a quick change in her demeanor. (Bullard) "She'll either wise up and finally get her act right, and realize you are the real thing in her life (and I have seen that happen by the way), or as I said in my story she'll just shrug her shoulders and be like *"Oh well, bye!"* as my former friend did when I told her off!" In that case guys, she was nothing to begin with anyway. She was using you the whole time, whether she was aware she was doing it or not. Black women, you better start checking yourselves! There are a lot of guys whose eyes are going to finally be open reading this book, and you better be ready for the aftershock when he finally confronts you! To all our strong black "good guys" out there, you are too much of a great guy to be anybody's seconds or safety net guy, cut her loose and move on!

5

The, Me, Me, Me! Mentality

So far we've covered the general problems of black women in chapter 1. We've discussed their conditional love terms in "The If Factor", as well as their constant need and desire to be mistreated in the "Masochistic Mind" and finally their sneaky tactics to have everything in "The Friend Factor". Now, we're going into the pure, selfish, self serving mentality that some black women have. This me, me, me mentality that black women can't seem to get over! This chapter in a lot of ways kind of co-insides with the other chapters of this book especially "The Friend Factor". This chapter kind of ties everything together; however, it looks at their selfishness at a broader scale than just relationships. But, this is where we will start since this is where we last left off.

Most black women have a *"what can I get out of it"* attitude when it comes to relationships. Everything they want is simply just about serving their own purposes, and not contributing to his life at all. Most successful black women are the worst! It seems when a black woman gets a little bit of success, money or status all of a sudden they have this **"checklist"** of all the things that he must have or be, otherwise he is disqualified from even talking to her. They don't want any man who doesn't have as much as they have or more, you hardly ever see a rich and successful black woman with a regular Joe. Even if they do get a regular guy, they will always hold their money and success over their heads like a guillotine for when ever he gets out of line. Sometimes, they'll be quiet about it but, as soon as they get into fight or argument her true feelings are going to come out, and she's going to let you know who's in charge, and who runs what! Most rich successful black women feel that a regular guy isn't good enough for them, and they will constantly remind you of that fact every single time you try to approach them. She's always giving you her resume (Bullard) "When I was dating this black woman who had a little bit of money and success, she was always telling me her credentials; *"I* *graduated with honors from my college, I was in the top five percent of my class, I make such and such a year, ain't nothing a man can get me I can't get for myself".* And, I'm thinking, damn why is she telling me all of this?! Who are you trying to convince me or you?! It was like I was at a job interview and she's giving me all these reasons why I should hire her".

The Equality Joke

No matter what profession they're in from, high profile lawyers, to C.E.O.'s of corporations, to business executives, to entertainers like singers and actresses, and don't get us started on these female rappers!! Black women scream equality, but only want it when it's convenient for them. You see it everyday, black women always want to be treated equal to men. They want all the perks and opportunities of being a man, but when it comes to facing the consequences that men have to face **then** they want to be treated like a woman! They always want to nag and argue when things aren't going they're way, and will say and do anything to push your buttons. Many won't stop till you've reached your breaking point, some even going as far as to hit you, but as soon as you hit them back then all of a sudden **you are the bad guy!!** *"How could you put your hands on me?"* *"I'm a woman"* They shout, knowing good and damn well some of them deserve it! Now we know we've lost a lot of you right there on that comment, because you guys have all been taught that under no circumstances is there a reason to hit a woman, even our own parents have instilled that in us, but can we be real for a moment?

People are always saying *"there's never an excuse to hit a woman"* but let us remind you that, that's only half true! The truth is you shouldn't put your hands on **anybody period!** But let's be honest here, some women actually push men emotionally to that level of physical violence, and there's a reason to hit anybody given the proper circumstances whether **male** or **female!** Black women just use that age old saying to get away with a lot of the things they do, like disrespecting men any kind of way, putting their hands on them, vandalizing their car, calling their moms bitches, etc. And, they know they can get away with it because, they have that excuse behind them (and the police department too!). A woman will do all kinds of physical things to a man and nothing will really happen to her, but as soon a he puts his hands on her **here come the cops!!!!** And, what's the cops all time favorite line they always use? *"You could have handled it better than that!"* **what kind of shit is**

that?! How the hell else are we supposed to handle somebody hitting us? Now, we don't want any of you to get the idea that we promote beating women, or any type of abuse. We're not saying that it's cool to hit women, nor do we support any type of domestic abuse. But, the point we're trying to make is when you attack his masculinity in any way, he's going to get defensive on you, sometimes to the point of physical violence! So watch how you approach these men black ladies! And, black men don't just up and hit them for any reason at all, but if they rise up to you like a man, remind them **real quickly** that they're not!

Let us ask you something black women, if men get their asses whooped, and children get their asses whopped, even dogs get their asses whooped, what makes you any different or better than us? Then there's this other age old saying *"Well you should've just walked away"*, but again let's be real! **It's just some stuff you can't just walk away from!!!** Don't be a woman when it's convenient for you!! Be equal all the time! If you buck up to man with your chest sticking all out like a guy, expect to get beat down like one!!!!

Users and abusers

You are the most ungrateful, unappreciative group of women who ever existed! Nothing you do for a black woman is ever good enough for them. A man could be taking care of a black woman (and her kids!), giving her money, paying her bills, etc, but the moment she gets angry or the two of them get into a fight about something the first thing that comes out of the black women's mouth is *"you don't do shit for me!"* Nothing satisfies them, and you wonder why so many black men are leaving these black women for other women or just leaving period! That man is trying as hard as he possibly can for you, and yet you keep dogging him out, and complaining, nagging and making it more frustrating for him! He can't get any type of peace in his house, and that's why you have so many men that never go straight home after work! Some of them go to bars and get a drink, or somewhere to watch a game, or over their friends house, hell, some just drive around until they know their woman or wife has gone to bed! And, that's just sad. A man's house should be a place of peace and serenity. A place where he can go and rest his head and get his mind right, and you black women should be doing everything you possibly can to make that happen for him! You, of all people should know how hard it is to be a black man in society and the stress it can cause! He shouldn't have to go all these places to get his head straight, it's his house, he should do it there!!

A man will go where he thinks he can have peace, and that's why a lot of men don't come straight home after work or after a business trip. He's been fighting, and putting up with bullshit all day long, and now he has to come home and do it there too?! That's why so many black men are so stressed out and dying young, did you know the average black man dies at 54? There having heart attacks and strokes, and stress attacks because he can't get **any** peace **anywhere!!** And personally we blame black women for this. **That's right we said it!!! It's your fault!!!** Black men are running themselves into an early grave dealing with these ungrateful, unappreciative black women who honestly just ain't worth the effort in our opinion anyway! If you like being around them, then you're crowding them! If you give them space, then you're not spending enough time with them! If a man is strong he's domineering, if he's sensitive she says he's weak, if he's accommodating then he's whipped and you run all over him! And, if he does something she usually does, then she says he can't do it as well as she can! Well the **"good"** black men are sick of this shit! We're sick of the nagging, the complaining. We're sick of taking the bullet for the last guy you were involved with because he dogged you out! You knew he wasn't shit when you met him but you screwed him anyway because you thought it was **"exciting"** at the time, and now you got a lunatic for a baby daddy, now you wanna sit there and say *"Men ain't shit!"* GROW THE HELL UP!!!!! No black man or any other man for that matter can be all these things at once, you need to choose what the hell it is you want and live with it!!!

Contradicting and Impatient

Black women are extremely contradictory, and extremely impatient. They say they want a successful man but when a man is out there on his grind trying to maintain his success and status they complain about it. They'll say *"you're never around!"* and *"why you always working so much?"* or *"you're not paying me enough attention!"* Then some of them have the nerve to cheat and use these reasons as an excuse! They want all the perks of being with a baller, but are not willing deal with what he has to go through to keep these things. All you saw was the "cars" and the "houses" and the "shine" (that's jewelry!), well it takes a lot of time and energy to maintain all of that, probably more than it took to get it! So don't contradict yourself by saying you want this type of man, and then complain when he's out grinding, trying to maintain all these things your gold digging ass was attracted to him for in the first place!

As far as them being impatient, they will not deal with a man that's trying to come up and better themselves the **RIGHT WAY!** They won't stand by the good one's at all, the ones that may work two jobs, sometimes three, to pay their way through school. Or just working the 9 to 5 shift, but is in transition to get a better position so his money's a little tight at the moment. But, they will give the bad one's all the chances in the world! That drug dealer, or gang banger, or that two bit hustler that's in the streets all the time, they'll stick with him till the end of the earth! Even if she does decide to stick with the good one, she will complain and **complain** that he's not coming up fast enough! Success takes time and you have to be willing put in the work and the time with him, **without complaining!!!!!** If not, what the hell are you in this for? If that good straight arrow guy isn't getting "his" fast enough she'll drop him in a heartbeat for the next baller that comes along (usually a drug dealer, pimp, gang banger or professional athlete) her way. She'll leave you in the wind and won't give a damn how you feel about it!! Then, the baller she left you for is the same type of asshole we spoke of in the previous chapters of this book, the one that treats you like dirt, and that's the one she'll remain loyal to!!!! She'll give him chance, after chance, after chance, and give every excuse under the sun for sticking with his ass! (Douglas) "My God, the whole thing is mind-boggling!!!"

The Greed of Black Women

Some black women have dated as many as 5 to 6 even 10 different guys just to get money and gifts for themselves. As we said in the "Friend Factor" some have friends for sex, you have your rent man, and even your food man, someone to take them out when they're short on money or just don't feel like paying for it. But, you sit there and have the nerve to call us "players" and "dogs" it seems to us that the word "bitch" and "ho" and "skank" do sometimes apply!! Many will try to even get pregnant by men on purpose just to get taken care of (and this is the only time mind you when a black woman will **TRY** to get pregnant by a man, seeing that most African American female pregnancies are unplanned. That's why a lot black women are so angry, and short, and half take care of the kids they have, because they didn't want them in the first place! They were just a "screw gone wrong", "raw sex at the wrong time"! To the kids reading this we know this may hurt your feelings but it is the truth. If you don't believe us just ask your mothers!)

Even if you do provide for her and your child, she can't wait to get to that court house to put you on child support! Let's get this straight, child support was made for the fathers who refused to take care of their children, so the government made a way to make them pay. If a man is being a good father to his kid, taking him to the doctor, buying what his baby or child needs, spending quality time with him, doing everything he's supposed to be doing as a father and a man whether he's with you or not, why the hell would you put him on child support anyway?!! We'll tell you why, it's just sheer **GREED** plain and simple!! Many black women have gone as far to put a baby on a man that isn't even the father on child support, and you black women sit there, cheer and clap and hi-five each other like you've won some type of victory or something. No wonder we have so much animosity toward you, and why many of us stop dealing with you altogether and disrespect you the way we do! Well, there it is black women right in your faces the way we really feel about you. So what are you going to do about it? Nothing as usual, right about now you black women who are reading this book we know your blood is boiling and you're filled with so much anger right now you don't know what to with yourself, but that's too damn bad. **THE TRUTH HURTS DOESN'T IT?** This shit has gone on for too damn long and enough is enough!!!! (And believe us black women we're not through with you yet!!!!)

If no other black men have the courage to stand up and say something we will! Black men read this book over and over again let it become your bible (along with the Holy Bible of course!) and use it to guide you through the good black women and the other types we described in this book. Yes, there are some good black women out there who are good to there men, and take care their business, and don't give him problems. They even actually agree with what we're saying in this book, you women had better start speaking up! These other "sistas" of yours are making the whole flock of you look bad. We're not talking about all of you, and if it seems we are believe us that's not our intention, and we're sorry. But somebody has got to speak up for the good black men out there getting screwed over for no good reason; someone has to fight for them!

We are making these topics known because we are not the only ones that feel this way. Turn on your television; you see it all the time in movies, talk shows, stand up comedy you name it. Someone's speaking out on it, maybe not as blunt, and as coarse as we are but it's still being said. And, maybe it needs to be said this way, it seems no other way seems to be working so being just out right blunt and raw will spark some kind of change in black women.

The Judgment and Prejudice of Black Women

Black women have a real bad problem being too prejudice, and when we say this we don't mean in the racial sense. The word prejudice literally means to "pre-judge" something or someone, or a situation before understanding completely about it. Before they even meet a man or sit and talk with him they've already made up in their minds who he is and what he's about. If he's dressed a certain way, they automatically suspect the worst of him with out even knowing him. Many men especially black men have been turned away or put down by black women simply because he didn't fit the description of her "checklist" for a perfect man. You don't know anything about that man, who knows? He could've been everything you wanted in a man but you'd never know because your stuck up asses refuse to get off your high horse and give him a few minutes off your time.

Then there's the issue of being too judgmental. This issue here is one of many reasons why black women are losing their men! It's like we do **one** thing wrong, and you crucify us for it!! They never let us forget it! In any and every argument we have she'll always bring it up! It could've been five years ago, but black women will just keep rehashing it! We're not condoning what they did or saying that you shouldn't be angry with him, but at some point you've got to let it go!!! It's like you black women keep this score card of everything we've done to you, and you constantly put it in our faces when we do anything wrong or get into some type of argument with you. **CUT US A BREAK!!!** We're not perfect and neither are you!!! Contrary to popular belief women have **WAY** more secrets than any man ever will, and care more about there self image than we do! Don't believe us? Why do you black women (or any other woman for that matter!) lie about how many men you have slept with? Regardless of what you've heard gentlemen, you haven't heard the true amount of what she's told you! Because she doesn't want to be labeled as a ho, as we said earlier, you always want to be equal, so why not tell the truth about it?! Women are always complaining *"When a man sleeps around, he's a player, but, if a woman does it she's a ho"* why? **Because, it's a man's world that's why!!** Like it or not we make the rules, and there are different rules that apply to men and women, and that's just the truth! Is it a double standard? **YES IT IS!** Why do you want to be us so bad then get mad when we call you out on it?! If you want to be like us you got to be able to take the heat like us, other wise get back in a woman's place!!! There are just some things we can do that you can't, just like there are certain things you can do that we can't, or we would get criticized and put down just like you! So, black women stop pleading equality because the truth of the matter is, there isn't any!!!

6

The Pride Factor

We've covered a lot of ground in this book, but now we're going to talk about the one subject that ties everything we have said from the previous chapters in this book together ... Pride. In this chapter we will discuss the unrelenting pride that black women have, the one trait that will be their complete undoing, if they don't change their ways. Everything in this book we have said so far believe it or not black women already know about it. They know about their attitudes, and their sneakiness, their prejudice and judgmental ways, and most of all there constant need to have and cause drama in the lives of other people especially black men. But, the saddest part of all this is not the fact that they know all these things we just mentioned, but that they know it and just **don't care!!!**

We give black women too much credit for being these finger snapping, neck rolling, attitude having women, like that's some kind of good trait! A lot of popular figures like comedians and entertainers (male entertainers) truly need to stop glorifying this kind of behavior. You see it a lot in some comedians routines (male and female) they make their behavior into something funny and it is for the most part, but all comedy is derived from some truth it's just exaggerated a little bit to make you laugh. A lot of actors and actresses try to make it seem like its something that promotes strength. They will say things like *"Oh she's just being a sister"* or *"She's just being a strong black woman"*, but listen, true strength is silent, it doesn't have to brag or boast, or belittle others, and real independence like true success speaks for it's self! Take Oprah Winfrey for instance, Oprah is one of the richest most powerful women on the planet. She's got clout, properties and connections most people dream of, but, you never see Oprah snapping her fingers and rolling her eyes, being all loud and obnoxious saying how she don't need a man and *"what ever a man can get, I get for myself!"* She carries her self with class and poise, and her success and strength speaks for itself! She doesn't have to shout to the world she's independent because we all know it! (Bullard) **"A class act!"** Men are not blind and they are not stupid, if you are all these things we mentioned it will show and radiate out of you.

It doesn't take a rocket scientist to see and notice that you've got it going on, or you're capable of taking care of yourself. You don't have to throw it in our faces every time you see fit! It has gotten so bad to the point that black women don't have to say it anymore it just exudes out of you like bad perfume. Fellas, you know what we're talking about, you see a nice looking black woman walking down the street, she's dressed nice, she's got her hair done, she looks like she's got it together, but the way she carries herself already turns you off! She's got this *"don't approach me unless you got something"* look about herself, and kind of scoffs at guys that are checking her out, and instantly you're turned off! That isn't cute, it isn't attractive and who the hell said it was sexy to act that way?!

Too Proud To Beg

A black woman will let her man go before they make any effort to get him back. Even if they know **they** were in the wrong!!!! It could be completely her fault, but she won't make any type of effort to get him back at all! She'll say stuff like *"You wanna leave? Fine, go ahead, leave go on get out!!"* They will not even **try** to make amends or plead their case with the guy or say *"Baby, I messed up please don't go, I'll do anything to make it better just don't go!!!"* Now a lot of black women would say that is called begging, and you know what ... it is!!! **But so what?!!!** Now we know what you've all been taught, what you're parents, your friends and everyone else you know have always said since you were little up till you were grown. *"Girl don't you beg anybody, I don't care if it is your fault, I don't care what happened, if he wanna leave, let him leave!"* But, that's only half true. If he's being a jerk or an immature child about the relationship or the situation, and decides he wants to throw a tantrum, or thinks he's going to teach you a lesson by walking out and/or stops calling you **then** you don't beg because you don't have time for that bullshit! If he can't be a mature man and handle the situation like an adult should, then by all means let his ass walk out, because you ain't missing anything anyway! But, when he's a good man and **you know** you're wrong and you haven't been doing the things you should have been doing (not spending time with him, cheating on him, taking advantage of his kindness, not appreciating the things he does for you.) and he gets tired of you and walks out, you ought to do what ever the hell you can to bring him back through that door! **Beg, shout, scream, cry**, do what ever you have to, to get him back!

Now, we know what a lot of you black women who are reading this book right now are thinking to yourself, saying out loud, or saying to your friends *"Oh **hell** no!!!, I'm not going through all that just to keep a man."* But, listen, there aren't that many good men out there, **you're** always saying that! You **finally** get one that's got some sense, treats you right, really loves you, and what do you do? You cut up, act a fool, cheat on him, or just keep him as your **"friend"** knowing that he likes or loves you. When he finally gets sick of you (as he should!) and walks out, you just sit there with your arms crossed and nose in the air and say *"SO!"* but, that ain't nothing but pride baby! Then you've got the nerve to breakdown and cry, just fall apart as soon as he walks out! You're calling all your friends and family boo-hooing and sobbing saying *"He just walked out and didn't say anything!"* Well, you didn't say anything to keep him there, so why should he stay?!! (Bullard) "Do you possibly think that, that **could've** been the reason why? I mean he walked out and he probably thought to himself, *"Well, shit! She didn't even attempt to try and make me stay, or talk me out of it, so it must mean she didn't care in the first place!"* And, even though she may not have meant that, the fact that she didn't say anything, that's how he took it!!!

It takes more strength to submit than it does to walk away. It takes more strength to follow than it does to lead. In a country that thrives off of "individualism" people seem to have gotten away from that. Black women think that having pride and **"standing your ground"** no matter what is a sign of strength, but it is only a sign of foolishness. You're going to let the best thing in your life walk away because you're out to prove some "point" that you don't need anybody and you're not begging anybody to stay around if they don't want to! To all you independent women out there, you finger snapping, neck rolling, *"sista girls"* who are driving away your men, you all think it's cute, you think it's funny! You slap hands and hi-five each other at the beauty salons, and workplaces, bragging about how you played him, and dissed him, and walked away from him, all the time not realizing that you're **losing the good men!!!!** Losing them to alcohol, to drug use, to depression, to suicide, to heart attacks, to strokes, to hypertension, **other men, WHITE WOMEN!!!** (Oh yes! We went there on you, and we're going to go further in the next chapter too!) And the saddest most heart breaking part of all this is,

you don't care!!! You don't care if he walks away, you don't care if he goes on the down low, you care if he goes outside his race, **YOU DON'T CARE IF HE DIES!!!** Good men die all the time fighting for these sorry, trifling, no good, ungrateful, unappreciative, attitude having, black women and nobody's fighting for them! Nobody's giving them the credit they deserve, nobody's patting them on the back for anything, and it's **sickening!!!!** He's losing his mind! He doesn't know what to do with his self anymore; he's done everything he can think of to make this woman happy!! He's tried everyway he knows how to make this woman see how much he loves her and cherishes her (in spite of her flaws!!). He's confused, he doesn't know what works for him anymore, what we call good, we now call bad, what we call bad, we now call good! Since when did going to school, and getting your education, and staying **out** of trouble, and, **not** dealing drugs, and **not** going to jail **make you a punk?!!** And, don't you black women dare sit there applaud and nod your head at that statement, because you're the main ones supporting these jackasses that do the exact opposite of what we just said!! You're out there treating prison like it's some kind of right of passage, like some badge of honor, **THE DEVIL IS A LIE!!!!!!!!** It is a curse, a curse of twisted logic, and bad judgment and we bind it in the name of Jesus!!!!

Black women; let us ask you a question, the ones out there dating these thugs, and hoodlums, and these spineless mama boys. Men you know do you wrong, but you stay with them any way because you think it's **"exciting"** or the women who can't seem to get control of your maternal instincts, let ask you, is it worth your life? Is it worth your peace of mind? Is it worth watching your daughters grow up thinking it's okay for men to call them "bitches" and "ho's", or letting some loser negro with **no** job and paying **no** bills move in with them and taking care of there rusty behinds all because they can **"lay pipe"?!** To all you independent women, is it worth being alone for the rest of your life, because you're so hell bent on proving you don't need him or anyone and now you've driven him away, and no one wants you because, honestly **it's just not worth the hassle?!** To all you women out there, going with these weak ass men you got to baby, and nurture, and always have to play the lead role in the relationship, because you can't seem to control your maternal instincts, and you think you're going to take half a man and raise him to be the man you want. (Bullard) ("I believe you're the most frustrated out of all of the rest, because you can't seem to get past the fact that your love is not strong enough to change him or any man for that matter! And, as we said in the "Masochistic mind" you're not raising any kids. He's either going to be a responsible man or he's not, you have no control over that!") Is it worth your peace of mind? You date and marry these spineless characters because they do what you say when you say it, and then you get mad and frustrated because he won't lead or make one decision around the house. **Well whose fault is that?**

The Hypocrisy of Black Women

Most black women are the most hypocritical women in the world! They say one thing but completely do another, Case in point, all these black women talking about how their being disrespected in all these rap videos and in hip-hop music, yet their the first ones dressing up like "hoochies" and "ho's" whenever they even **hear** of a video shoot being shot somewhere in their area! They do these TV specials on how they are portrayed and how their viewed and how it portrays black women in a negative light. Look! No rapper, producer, or video director is putting a pistol to your heads making you go down to these video shoots and dress like this, and act like video ho's!! If it's so offensive and so degrading **THEN STOP TAKING YOUR ASSES TO THE AUDITIONS!!!!!!** Stop blaming hip-hop, stop blaming the rappers that sing these songs, stop dressing like a skank, and stop dancing at the clubs when the songs come on!!!! Anybody's who's been to a club knows that the black women are the main one's on the floor dancing to the nastiest, most freakiest, most degrading songs that's out there!!! **And black women don't even try to deny it!!!!** And, for any skeptics out there who don't believe us, just go to a club and see for yourself!!!

If you want to kill a movement or stop a product, you don't stop the **supply** you stop the **demand!!** You black women keep dancing and dressing up like **"ho's"** and **"sluts"** at the clubs and going to these video shoots looking like you look, so it must not be too degrading!! We know what a lot of you black women who are in the entertainment business are saying *"Well, we gotta work; we're just trying to get our foot in the door!"* But, there are other ways to get your foot in the door baby, so don't give us that lame excuse!! Of course there are exceptions to the rule. There are some women that have to strip or dance because they're out of options and because of special circumstances and conditions in their life, so they're just doing what they got to do. But for the most part this isn't the case! Why do you dress like a slut, walk like a slut, talk like a slut, act like a slut, **THEN GET MAD WHEN WE CALL YOU**

A SLUT?!!!!! To all these rappers and any one else in the hip-hop business, if these black women are so offended and appalled by the way they're portrayed in these videos then **stop hiring them!** That will just solve all your problems, but then again it probably won't because then they will complain that they don't hire enough black women in the videos and it's **"discrimination"**, well listen, you're the only group of women complaining and making so much of a fuss about the situation! Other races don't have anywhere as near as much to say about it as you all do, so either deal with it, or **SHUT THE HELL UP ABOUT IT!!!**

(Douglas) "A very popular talk show hostess who's an ex-supermodel did a show on exotic dancers. She spoke of them as if they were degrading themselves for choosing this profession for their lives. She even went undercover as an exotic dancer but lacked the courage (surprise, surprise!) to go on stage and perform after all that huff and puff she talked about on her show about how she was going to! She felt that she could never expose her body and degrade her self in such a way. How can she say that when she was one of the top lingerie and swimsuit models in the world?!! She's taken more provocative photos than most supermodels have. I know a lot of people are saying that exotic dancing and modeling are two different things but **exposure is exposure!** Now what's that say about her? That she's a hypocrite **plain and simple!** And you can **BANK** on that!!!!" Also these female bashing songs are just the same way. Especially that "No Scrubs" song that was all the rave several years ago! How the hell are you gonna make a song that pertains to you as well? All these women talking about *"I don't want no scrub, I don't want no scrub!!!"* You're as broke as he is but you wanna sing that song?" (Bullard) "You also have the other songs like "Earls in the trunk" and that **real** popular song "Think before he cheats". Women make all these songs about doing these sadistic twisted things to men, but as soon as a man was to make a song like that **HE'S CRAZY!!!!** Hypocritical bullshit! All of it!" Most of you women, black and other wise don't know what the hell you want! What the hell a good man is, or how to treat one, so go somewhere and sit down!!!

The Anger of Black Men

We're not prophets in any way, or do we pretend to be any type of geniuses. We're not preachers, or statistical experts or doctors of any kind. We're just regular guys who have witnessed and experienced enough problems with black women in our (and other people's) lives. Enough problems to finally get angry about it and do something. Black men all across this country are angry, though you black women may not see it or know it because you're so caught up in your own problems and issues and **"careers"** that you don't see the fact that, that the good black men are **angry** and **frustrated** and they are **tired!** He is tired of giving so much and getting so little in return! He is tired of always having to flex up and fight and be this hardcore person, that doesn't have any problems or issues, because that's what he was raised to do!! We all were raised to be these strong emotionless beings! To never cry, to never show, weakness, to just take what ever comes our way and to shut up and deal it with, because *"You're a man!! And men don't talk about their feelings!!" "Suck it up!!"* is what they all say *"That's life!!!" "Be a man and deal with it!!"*

Well, we're tired of having to **"deal with it!"** we're tired of always having to be "Superman" for you, and you not see it or appreciate it! Angry and frustrated lovers and husbands dying or leaving because they are tired and worn out and they sit and wonder what happened to the dream that was in their life? They spent all this time trying to appeal to this woman who wanted this lifestyle, and this house, and this car, and he got so caught up in it all that he forgot the dream that was in his heart. Black male celebrities and pro-athletes are angry because they have to spend their whole life walking on eggshells and watch everything they do, because their "role models" and people are looking up to them! Well, who the hell said they wanted to be looked up to? All they want to do is play the game, make music, and make movies. They really don't give a shit how your life turns out, hell; your life is what you make it!! Why is it that when people make it big, get rich, or become famous, that all of sudden they have something great or important to say?! It puts undo pressure on the celebrities and athletes! They're human just like me and you, and all they want to do is live their life! They're tired of getting blamed for your kids cutting up acting a fool, because of your **LACK OF PARENTING SKILLS**, and your failure to separate **entertainment from reality**!! The truth is you do it to make yourselves feel better and absolve yourselves of any responsibility!!

Married men are angry because they feel they didn't get what they gave, single men are angry because, they can't seem to find the right woman that will appreciate them for who they are! You black women are always saying you want a good man, **he's there, he's right there in front of you!!!** But, you just don't see it or accept it and he is **ANGRY!!!** Angry because he sees you going through these problems and situations, and heartbreaking after heartbreaking relationship, and he's watching you cry and cry and say **"Why won't any man love me?!!!!"** and he's yelling back at you at the top of his lungs through what he does, and his availability, and it's even him sometimes just telling you **"I'M RIGHT HERE!!! I'M RIGHT HERE!!! I LOVE YOU!!! I WANT YOU!!! I NEED YOU!!!! I'VE BEEN TELLING YOU THAT ALL THIS TIME WHY CAN'T YOU HEAR ME?!!!!"** But, you still don't hear him and continue to go about your daily routine, and he is angry to the point that he has become resentful and bitter, because he is tired and frustrated, and he is drained! He has run out of himself because he gave so much and never got it back, now he has to fight depression and stress because you left him hanging and didn't think twice and he feels that no one cares, and he can't express himself the way he wants to because after all, he's been trained (like we all have) since birth to *"suck it up"* and *"don't cry"* and *"don't tell anyone because it's a sign of weakness"* and, after all, *"what will other people say?!" "What will my woman say?!" "What will my wife say and think?!" "What will women in general say and think about me?!"* He doesn't feel he has anyone to turn to and talk with without being judged so he turns to the only place he feel he can go and not be judged … the strip club, the hookers on the street, the brothels in certain cities.

You may have laughed at that last statement black women, but let us assure you, if you actually pulled a hooker, or a stripper, or a call girl to the side you would be **AMAZED** at the stories you hear from them. Men paying hundreds to even thousands of dollars to just **talk!!** They don't want sex, they don't a blow job, they just want to **talk** to someone who'll listen and **not judge them**, and not criticize them, and not tell them **"well you should have known better!!!"** and **"what the hell's the matter with you?!!"** and **"don't you have any sense at all?!"** Men don't want to hear all that! Contrary to what you believe men are way tougher on themselves than any woman will ever be! You can't beat him up any more than he's already beaten him self up! So just shut up, and listen to what he has to say! He's your man; you're his lady. The two of you are supposed to be best friends and confidants as well as lovers. If he can't turn to you who can he turn to? Because we guarantee you black women, he's gonna turn **somebody!!** And, if you don't get off your judgmental high horse, and let him express himself freely our question is **who are you sending him to?!!!!**

What you're saying, and what we are Hearing

A lot of times what you're saying and what we're hearing, or how we're taking it are two different things. You may say something to us, but we may here something totally different. Something you think is funny and cute, and don't think much of it, could be something that destroyed your whole relationship or communications with him, and now your relationship or marriage is in turmoil because you shot your mouth off! For example; a man comes home and says *"Baby, I lost my job. They laid me off!"* You may say something like *"Damn! What the hell did you do to get laid off?!"* Now, you may not think that what you said was offensive or even accusatory, but let us tell you how he probably heard it; He heard *"Dammit negro, can't you do anything right? I know you probably said or did something to lose your job, and now I got to go screw someone else!"*

You probably think that that last remark was some what comical, but let us assure you even though you didn't literally **"say"** all that, that's what he heard. You have to understand that he's at an impasse right now, one of the things he prides himself on is providing for those he loves. His ego is very fragile right now and you have to watch what you say to and around him. Here's what you should have said; *"Aw baby, it's okay! You're one of the strongest most intelligent men I know, I'm sure you'll find another job soon, why don't we search together?!"* You see? A statement like that would put him in a totally different mind state. It'll believe it or not give him more motivation than ever. *He'll think "Man, she really believes in me! She doesn't think, she knows I can get out there and find another job. I'm gonna try even harder to get on somewhere else!"*

Another example; is when you're making love and he's not hitting the spot right or not doing what it takes to get you off the right way, and on top of that he finishes too quick! He's already embarrassed and tired, and all he can say is *"I'm sorry baby!"* What do you do? You give him one of those reassuring pats on the cheek or face and half a smile and roll over and go to sleep. In this case it's what you **don't** say that can get you in trouble. Because you didn't say anything he's probably thinking; *"Oh so what you trying to say?! That I have a small penis?! That I can't hit the spot right and make that right leg twitch?!* **WHAT YOU TRYING TO SAY?!!!!!** What you should do is sit him down and tell him what gets you off and excited! But, here's the trick, you got to tell him in a way that's going to get him motivated. Something like; *"Baby, you know what really gets me off and horny is when you do (fill in the blank). "My God, it drives me nuts when you (fill in the blank).* Saying it like that will light a fire under his ass and he will go all out to try to make you reach that "O" haven!

The Curse of Independence
The Burden of Having a Good Man

(A Theory by Hank Bullard)

"I'm going into a subject here that may very well be very controversial in its content, but it's something that needs to be talked about and discussed nonetheless. Through my own experiences and witnessing the experiences of people close to me, I've come to learn that many black women say they want a good man, but the truth is a lot of black women can't handle it. I know we've discussed this in earlier chapters; however I'd like to take a closer look as to the "why" in this sub-chapter. A lot of times black women say *"I want a good man"*, but what exactly is a "good man"? Is it someone who pays the bills? Is it someone who keeps the lights on, pays the car note, has a good job or keeps a food on your plate? The actual answer is neither! The truth is he could be paying the bills, and still be neglecting you! Or paying the car note, and keeping food on your plate, but is still beating and abusing you physically and emotionally! Sometimes, he's keeping the lights on just so he can see where to hit you!

A lot of times we confuse these things as being a "good man". Women say *"Oh, he has two jobs!"* or *"He's a hard worker!"*, or *"He goes to church, everyday!"* (**So does the Devil!**) And, you automatically say or think *"He's a good man"*. But, I want to challenge this way of thinking for a lot of you black women. You often say you want a "good man" without really knowing what it is you're asking for. The fact of the matter is having a good man is actually more of a burden, than having a bad one! I know that's a paradox, if you've ever heard one, but please just hear me out. It's a lot like saying *"freedom isn't free"* sounds paradoxical too I know, but the truth is freedom cost you something. Look back at your life at the time you were growing up. Your easiest time was when you lived with your parents. You were told what to, how to do it, when to go to bed, a curfew for when you had to be in. I know you hated it, because I hated it too! Because, we wanted our freedom so bad! *"No one tells me when to come in!"* we say to ourselves, *"No one tells me what to do!!"* we shout aloud!

But, look what happens when you finally do move out. You're now actually more stressed out than you we're when you lived at home with you're parents! *"Why is that?"* you ask? Because the burden of freedom has been bestowed upon you! Listen people, the absence of dependability is responsibility! I know that this is a book and you could read that phrase again, but I'll repeat myself anyway **the absence of dependability is responsibility!** Just like darkness is the absence of light! I know the phrase "The burden of freedom" sounds like a paradox, but let's examine this phrase for a minute. When you lived at your parent's house you were under someone else's rules and regulations, but ultimately they were responsible for you. You didn't have to worry about rent because it was covered, you didn't have to worry about food, because it was provided, and you didn't have to worry about the lights going out either, because it was paid for. Basically, you had no responsibilities, because ultimately they were responsible for your well being.

But, the moment you moved out, you became responsible for yourself, and for a lot of you who first move out that's a tough thing! It's tougher because the penalty is now higher for you if you're not responsible! If you don't pay rent, you're gonna be homeless! If you don't work you don't eat! And if you don't pay your power bill you will be in the dark and your food will spoil. Moving out forces you to take a look within yourself, because responsibility and accountability are issues from within, and the bottom line is that's what it's all about anyway! I know, and you know we've all asked ourselves the question; *"Do I have what it takes to move out? To truly live on my own?!* Because, you and I both know people who moved out stayed gone less than a year and then moved back in with their parents, or got evicted, or couldn't keep the lights on, because the truth of the matter is the weight of responsibility and accountability was too much for them! Because of issues and problems they had going on with themselves, they were not able to withstand the true weight of freedom. And, while the **IDEA** of being on their own and having a place to call their own sounded good to them, the truth is they can't handle it when they get it, because the freedom is forcing them to pull something out of them that isn't there!

When you have a good man, I mean a **REALLY** good man!! He's got his stuff together, he doesn't cause drama, and he's polite, respectful, considerate, and responsible!! He doesn't need help handling his business because he's got it under control, he doesn't have any kids and has good credit, I'm talking about **A REAL MAN BABY!!!!!** When you're actually face to face with a man like that, most black women turn tail and run in the other direction. The reason for this is that **true goodness, like true freedom demands responsibility and accountability!** The sheer goodness of that man will cast a reflection back at yourself as if someone were holding a mirror to your face, forcing you to look at yourself! **And if it's one thing that people hate doing, it's looking at themselves!!** Being forced to confront their own fears and insecurities, and being forced to ask that same question we all ask ourselves when we taste true freedom or goodness; *"Do I have what it takes to handle true freedom or goodness?"* Or the bigger question a lot of you black women ask yourselves when you actually do get a **truly good** man; *"Do I deserve it?"*

The truth is having a good man is way more demanding, requires more work, and is much more stressful than having a bad one! Because as I said earlier, it forces you to look within to pull something out of you that may not be there! And rather than deal with that, it's much easier to be with the trifling man, or the hoodlum, or the spineless mama's boy, because it relieves you of the **responsibility** of having to **correct yourself!!** It sets you free of being **accountable** for your own faults, inadequacies and inequities! And, it makes it much easier for you to put the blame on the trifling hoodlum and say; *"It didn't work out, because he blah, blah, blah!"* It's a lot easier and takes less strength to let things fall apart than it does to hold them together! And, as we said earlier, you know when a good man likes you, or is even in love with you, or has any feeling for you at all! But, yet you make up these sorry ass scapegoat excuses like *"he's too nice"* or *"he's boring!"*, but the actuality is he's not "too nice" or "boring" you're just **shallow** and **lazy!!!** By that, I mean there's not much to you, or there's not much inside of you that's gonna connect with him because you won't face yourself! And, in the presences of true goodness, you get scared and you panic and run back to the familiar, because you just saw yourself for who you truly are and you don't like it!! And, while the **IDEA** of having a good man sounds good to you, that's not really what you want, because you are **SELFISH**, by nature!!! **You** want, what **you** want, when **you** want it!! True love gives, and true lust takes! Don't agree? Just read the bible, it says that *"God, so loved the world that he **gave** his only begotten son"*, key word here is **GAVE!!!** True love demands sacrifice, true love demands change, and ultimately the biggest problem that most black women have, true love demands **SUBMISSION!!!** I know that just screwed up your independent mind right there, so I'll give you a moment to recover…. You done? Okay good, we can continue now."

7

Why Black Men Crossover

All right ladies and gentlemen we've discussed everything about the black woman from their many little problems and issues to, their selfish thinking, and arrogant pride. And, now we're going get to the reason (the real reason mind you, not the politically correct one!) why black men crossover to White Women, Asian Women, Mail Order Brides etc. Now, before we get started on this, we want to get a few things straight. We're not in any way saying that White Women, Asian, Latino, etc. are perfect! They have issues and problems just like black women, some even have that B.B.A (Black Bitch Attitude) we've been talking about throughout this whole book. But, for the most the most part when you compare the other races to black women, they are still practically perfect for companionship over them. The three of us are not just speaking from what we've seen and heard but through our own personal experiences as well.

First and foremost lets start with the obvious ... attitude. White women's attitudes are far better than black women's. They have a more of a *"What can I do for him"* attitude as opposed to black women's selfish *"What can he do for me"* attitude. Again, as we have said throughout the entire chapters of this book, this type of talk is often diluted in comedy routines, in a more light hearted manner, because no one wants to hurt anyone's feelings. But, we don't give a damn about your feelings! That what's wrong with the world today! Everyone's walking on egg shells, because no one wants to *"offend"* anyone or hurt anyone else's *"feelings"* and everyone wants to be liked and accepted, and no one wants to "rock the boat", but we're all about truth and that's what your going to hear in this book whether it hurts and offends you, or not!

Why?

Black women tend to wonder why it is so many black men (especially the rich ones!) tend to crossover to other races, especially white women. Well, there are so many reasons that they probably won't fit into this book, but we'll try to put in as many as possible. White women go the extra mile to support black men and keep a smile on their faces. They go above and beyond the call of duty (especially sexually). First of all, most white women will give just about any man a chance. You even see it in Hollywood, a lot of white female celebrities date normal, nine to five average Joes. Guys that don't have much, just your run of the mill guys who they like, and want to get to know. But even white women who are not celebrities, but are high profile women, C.E.O's, lawyers, corporate executives etc. (and we know from personal experience, not just from rumors or simple observation!) White women will even approach you and offer to buy you a drink at a club. They'll even ask you out and even pay for it! And, the big difference is there's no attitude, no arrogance about her, just a guy and a girl on a date just being together. They are willing to get to know a man before they pass judgment on him; they just have a more approachable personality. You can step to them without that fear of drama or confrontation that black women seem to give off. You can buy them a drink and they will actually sit there and kick it with you for a while. If they don't like you or don't want to talk to you they simply won't accept your offer to buy them a drink, no matter how bad they want it! (Bullard) "I have seen and experienced this for myself; they will give just a simple *"no thanks!"* or *"I don't think so!"* no attitude, no drama, no chance of any problems." Like we said in the first chapter in this book, if you don't like a man or are not interested in him don't accept any thing from him, no matter how bad you want it or need it!"

The Sexual Difference

One of the main differences that are between black women and white women that make black men cross over a lot is their sexual performance. While we have discussed throughout this whole book how black women have these rules, and stipulations about sex, and how they like to ration out sexual favors and acts. Well, one of the things that make **most** white women so different is that they don't have that issue! White women learn what it is you like sexually and they **do it!** Every time, all the time! Whatever it takes to keep their man or husband, even when it's something they may not like or particularly care for! (Bullard & Douglas) "We've heard white women say all the time, *"Well I don't like, or care too much for"* what ever sexual favor they're talking about, but then they will say *"But, my boyfriend (or husband) loves it when I do it!"* or we have even heard them say *"Well, I didn't like it at first, but as I got into it, I **REALLY GOT INTO IT** and now I love it!"* You see black women? When you give something a chance and try it, you never know you will end up liking or even loving it! And, not to mention the gratitude you will get from your man or husband for doing those things, even when you weren't into it. The fact that you were willing to do it anyway just to please him will earn you great favor with him!

Another great trait that white women have over black women, is that their more sexually expressive. White women are not afraid to say what it is they like or what they are sexually into. This cuts down on a lot of bullshit red tape conversation that you would have to have with black women before you get to the truth of what they like. A lot of black women bullshit, and dance around the issue of what they like sexually. Some of them even lie about it, only to find out later that they were into it! We've had countless conversations with white women, and the conversation just flowed. We talked about all kind of things so naturally, and the sexual conversation was **unbelievable!!!** There were no limits, no subject was taboo, and what was even greater is that we could ask them anything and there was no attitude, no turning up their nose, or looking at us funny, just real talk!

The Money Issue

A lot of black women ask *"Well, why is it that these black men date us, but when they come up and get rich, they go get white women?!"* Well, we'll tell you, because **having money gives you options, that's why!!!** There's an old saying that goes *"He who has the gold, has the power!"*, and as arrogant as that may sound, it's the truth! A man who has more money has more options, and therefore gets the pick of the litter. Black women are so attitudinal, and so opinionated, and just so hard to get along with, that most black men are sick of them. But, the fact that they are not as **"banked up"** as some ballers they feel that they can't do any better than what they have, so they tend to tolerate more bullshit than a guy that has a couple of millions in his account. You think a black man with money, and status is going to put up with some attitude having, finger snapping, black bitch, that always has something to say, and is never grateful for anything **and** is **sexually stingy?** As opposed to a white woman, or Asian woman, or any other race of woman who is sweet, but aggressive? Who knows their place and will stay in it? And, most of all is a **FREAK** and will do anything sexually anytime any way they want it with no attitude and a big smile on their face too?!!!

Money gives black men options, just like beauty give women options. You see it all the time, a fine ass, sexy woman doesn't have to take shit off any guy, because she knows that ten more guys are waiting in the background to take her out and be with her. So therefore, her attitude is more laid back; she's not worried about losing you too much, because her rolodex is full of guys that are ready to take her out. As opposed to an ugly woman who doesn't get much action, so she has to take what she get and hold on to it as best she can! She has **no choice** but go that extra mile for her man! She'll do things like cook, clean, come up to your job with lunch, her ugly ass had better bring you something to eat if she intends on keeping you! Now we know that all the pro-athletes and actors, and entertainers say the same cliché, politically correct thing when it comes to dating and marrying white women. They say that, "that's the only type of women in their social circle so that's who they always end up with". But we're here to tell you that's **GRADE A, BULLSHIT!!!!** They have that much money, that much clout, and practically can go anywhere in the world they want and have options out the ass, you mean to tell us you believe that?! They have access to black women but, the truth is they just don't want to be bothered with the drama!

The reality is there are certain things that a woman can do to attract a man whether he's married or single, or has a lady. There are certain things she can do to get him to react back or respond a certain way, as we said earlier we are not complex creatures. Things like, supporting a dream he has, no matter what it is. If a man comes to you and shares his dream with you, he wants to hear nothing from you but **encouragement!** No matter how ridiculous, insane or even stupid it sounds! If you cheer him on no matter what, he will keep you with him and by his side at all times. Even when he falls, if you're there to cheer him up, and tell him to get back in it, he will go further than you can ever imagine! We have seen countless black women destroy and put down so many black men's dreams because they want to inject what they call **"reality"** into the situation. They make little comments and suggestions toward their men or husbands that seem like their questioning their dream, or worse, their competence to carry it out! Black woman that's a **turn off!**

When some other woman comes along and supports him and cheers him on, and gives him praise on even the smallest progress, and is always saying *"you can do it baby!"* and he ends up sleeping with her, and having an affair with her you got the nerve to be all shocked and hurt! **WELL IT'S YOUR FAULT!!!** It's your fault; because you should have been supporting him from the get go! Men (like God) gravitate toward the loudest praise and cheer, whether it's from his wife or significant other, and like we said in the last chapter if you're not supporting him who are you sending him to?!! Black women here's a little friendly advice; if you don't support him, and his dream, and be his cheering section **someone else will!!!** Just like sexually you're always saying *"If you don't hit this right you'll find somebody who will!"* Well, that same rule applies to men when it comes to supporting him and his dream! Don't expect to enjoy in the spoils of his labor after you've bashed him down with your **"B.B.A"** all this time!

We hear so many black women say *"Just because he's got money, or is a celebrity, or plays pro ball, he thinks I'm supposed to be all up under him. Well I'm just not doing it!"* And that's just what we talked about in the "Pride Factor" in the last chapter. Other races of women say *"I'm gonna play to his ego and get in his head and be that submissive, subservient women, because the bottom line is the mission, and the mission is to get his money. So, what ever I gotta do I'll do it!"* You see black women?! If you're gonna be a gold digger at least be smart about it! And, finally, give him the kind of sex that **HE** wants, not the type of sex that you **feel like giving!!!!!** That's where you're losing a lot of your black men ladies!! (Bullard) "It's like buying a gift for someone you love. Most people hate their gifts because it's not what **they** want! The buyer bought something **THEY THOUGHT** would be nice for them, instead of what the person likes, so there in lies the conflict." You're giving him sex that **you** wanna give or what you **think** he should have or **deserves**, instead of what he likes!

(Bullard) "Imagine having a plant, you can love and admire that plant all you want. You can even say to it *"I love you"* and *"I care about you"*, but if you're not giving it what it needs for survival which is water and sunlight the plant will die! It doesn't matter what you say to it! Whether you love it, or hate it! Whether you tell it *"I love you"* or *"I hate your guts!"* If you're not doing what it takes to keep the plant alive and nourished it will die on you!" Black women you love these men and we truly believe you do, but the truth of the matter is you're not doing what it takes to nourish and take care of your relationship and it ends up dying! Like a plant needs the sun **and** the rain, you can't just give one thing and **not** give the other! You say *"Well I gave him some last night!"* But did you give him that 20 minute blow job that he loves so much?" Did you rub his back and talk dirty to him like he likes, or did you just give the same lazy 2 minute blow job that most couples and especially married couples give when they've gotten used to their man and the relationship? You say *"Well I went down on him!"* Yes! But, did you lick his balls? Oral sex is not just *"slurping the tool"*, but you gotta give his *"nutty buddies"* some attention too! And most of all, **STOP HAVING AN ATTITUDE ABOUT IT WHEN YOU DO IT!!!!!** So many black women do all these sexual things, but they do it with so much anger and frustration it's not worth the hassle of doing it! *"OKAY, FINE, I'LL DO IT DAMN!!!!!"* they say, then they'll slam their bodies over the couch or the bed bent over with their asses in the air saying: **"COME ON GET IT!!!!"** HURRY UP!!!!! SHIT!!!!** That's just as bad as you not wanting to do it!

We're not trying to be gross or tasteless here, but these are the hard core facts and truths that men feel and think about! Like we said in the intro, this book is written through a man's point of view and perspective. While you think the issues we have are minute and trivial we're saying to you **"that's what's making him leave!"** (Bullard) "If a woman fulfilled every sexual fantasy that her man or husband had when he wanted it, exactly how he wanted it, I mean every single **one** no matter what it was, **THERE WOULD BE NO PORNOGRAPHY!!!!!!"** You may argue with that statement, even disagree with it you're certainly entitled to your opinion just like Hank just stated his in his quote. But the fact of the matter is people watch pornography like movies; to provide some sort of escape one way or another in to some type of fantasy, but if they had that fantasy everyday in their homes, what the hell do they need to watch it on tv, when they've got it in their own house?!!!! Kinda defeats the purpose don't you think?

Mail Order Brides

The latest craze now a days are mail order brides, and while a lot of black men aren't really doing this, it's still a subject we thought we'd touch on as well. Too many men today are so scared of being called *"sexist"* or *"chauvinistic"* that they won't say the real reason why they get mail order brides, but we'll tell you! Men are getting mail order brides because they are tired of these independent, opinionated, career driven women, putting their jobs and career ahead of them or any one else! These women now a days act like the word **"housewife"** is some kind of curse word or something! Many men want the traditional, stay at home wife that's gonna keep her place and do what she's told! We can see all you black women's nose just turning up at that last statement but, **yes we said it!!** Let us men school you women on something for a brief minute, a man will choose his order and his peace before he chooses you! By that, we mean whether he loves you or not, that is completely irrelevant! If you're causing chaos (nagging and complaining) or getting out of line (trying to wear the pants or play the role of a man) he will get rid of you! That's why so many men are ordering mail order brides over the internet, or just choosing to date or marry overseas!

Every culture except North American women seem to respect the order of marriage and family, and don't mind letting a man be man and run things in his house. But like we said earlier this country thrives on "individualism" and everybody being their own person and walking their own path. Black women are always talking about how hard it is to be them and to do what they do, but let us tell you for one minute what its like to be us. First off, from the jump you expect us to be this solid wall of support, provision, and steadiness no matter what! You want us to be this "Superman", to work, pay bills, hold the family together, come to the rescue of everything and everybody and through it all we can't show one moment of weakness, emotion, fatigue, or even shed one tear or we're "weak" in your eyes! Being a man most of the time (especially dealing with black women) means that you always have to be "on" and never really getting the chance to be "off" or you'll look at us funny!! We know what you black women are saying or thinking right now; *"Well you're a man! You're supposed to be like that, you're supposed to provide and protect, and lead your family and handle everything* **THAT'S WHAT MEN DO!!!"** But, you would get mad as hell if we told you, *"You're supposed to cook, clean and have babies,* **THAT'S WHAT WOMEN DO!!!"** Although it would be the truth!!! Let us ask you something? Why is it that you can constantly remind us of our role, but we can't ever remind you of yours?!! Not only that, you get mad when we do?

Black women we have three options for you. Only three for you to choose from when a man tells you what he wants sexually and how he wants it! And what he expects out of a woman, and there's really no way around it either!

1.) You can cut him completely loose, and leave him alone! Just tell him *"Hey, baby I don't roll like that, maybe you need to find someone who does."* And that's fine no hard feelings!

2.) If you feel you have a good thing going and don't want to ruin the relationship. Allow him to get that specific thing he wants else where. Say *"Hey baby, if you feel you gotta get that so bad, just go ahead and do it! Just don't let me know about it! And don't disrespect our house by bringing them here!"* That's fine too, because some of you feel you gotta good man that has a specific want or need that you **know you ain't fulfilling**, so if he gets it somewhere else it's cool with you. Just be discreet about it!

3.) **SUBMIT!!!!** Swallow your **stupid ass pride**, and give in to your man's wants and desires. You just gotta say to yourself. *"Hey, I got a good man, and I'm not losing him over no bullshit! So I'm gonna swallow my pride, and do what I gotta do!"*

Those are the only three options you have black women, **PICK ONE!!!!!!!**

8

Sex: The Basic Foundation

By: Hank Bullard

Alright black women, we've covered so much so far about the behavioral patterns that you have (or in some cases don't have!) pride issues and etc. Now, I'm gonna try to break it down as simply as I can one more time to make sure you get the gist of what we're saying in it's entirety. As you have noticed a lot of subject matter we refer to in this book refers back to sex or sexual issues in some way shape or form. But, it's not because we're a bunch of out of control, oversexed, lust driven, perverts. The reason we revert back to the issue is for one simple reason: sex is one of the foundations of a man's nature. What, do I mean by that? What I mean is sex is basic, it's as basic as a hunger for food, a thirst for water, and it is as natural as breathing air. Let me give you a better example: A man is thirsty, he is in the desert. The sun is scorching his skin, his throat is dry, and he's been walking for hours. There's no water in the well at his home, because it's either gone dry or for some reason it's not producing like it use to anymore. So he leaves the comfort of his home to find somewhere to quench this basic need. He walks and walks, till finally on the verge of passing out he comes across this filthy ravine filled with the most unclean water you could imagine. Now, there's no water around for miles, and this man's on the verge of dying, so instinctively, without giving it a second thought he bends his knees and drinks from that filthy ravine. Did he know better? Yes he did! Did he have a better option? Certainly! But keep in mind that the well at home had gone dry and wasn't producing any more, or wasn't producing enough to satisfy his daily needs. So he had to take whatever was offered at the time.

A lot of you black women especially to all you *"fine sistas"* out there who can't figure out why your man cheated on your *"fine ass"* with a broad that looks like death warmed over, I'll tell you why! It's because you didn't satisfy his basic fundamental need!! You didn't give him what he wants, when he wants, for as long as he wanted it! You didn't produce at all or not enough of the one thing that was gonna keep him faithful to you, and he went to quench that thirst elsewhere! Did he know better? Yes he did! Did he have a better option? Certainly! But his source was cut off and/or didn't put out enough like she should've and now you sit there crying your eyes out, ready to cut somebody, when all of this could've been avoided if you had just done your job!

Men & Women the Sensuous Difference

To clarify also why men have a roving eye. I will also breakdown some simple principles for you to deal with as you ask yourself *"Why does my man/husband look at other women?"* and *"why isn't he attracted to me anymore?"* The **big** difference is this: **Men are stimulated by sight!** That's why God made the woman so curvy and gave her so many parts to be admired. Don't believe me? Where do you think all of the fetishes come from? You got breast men, thigh men, ass men, even foot men. Men that love long hair, and nice smiles, I mean it's a biological fact! **Women are stimulated by words!** Every guy in this world has been trained since they were kids to always tell a woman how pretty she is or give her some kind of compliment. Tell her how great dinner was, how nice her shoes are, even as a kid my dad used to always tell me, when he and my mom dressed up fancy to go somewhere *"Go in there and tell your mother how pretty she looks!"* or *"Go tell your sister she looks nice!"* *"Go thank your mom for dinner!"* Words stimulate a woman's mind just like sight stimulates a man's mind plain and simple!

Now, to tie all these strings together. Black women, you're always complaining about how *"He don't pay no attention to me anymore!"* and *"He's always looking at other women"* or *"He don't like to have sex with me anymore"* *"Why do men act like this?"* I'll tell you why; because for most of you black women you don't stimulate his sight anymore! You feel since you *"got the man"* now it's no longer a priority to look good to him anymore. You gain 80-90 pounds after you get married, you put on those lint covered pajamas! You know, the ones that your Grandma used to where! You don't come to bed sexy anymore, you don't **dress** sexy anymore, you dress *"comfortable"* now! You feel since you cook his food, clean the house, had his babies, are raising his kids and stuck with him when he was broke or *"wasn't shit"* as so many of you put it, that you're just automatically exempt form fulfilling his basic sexual needs. Completely ignorant to the fact that the same thing you did in the beginning to stimulate his sight which in turn activated his desire is the **EXACT SAME THING** you gotta do to maintain his stimulus and desire, so he can pay you the same compliments that stimulated your mind when you first met him! **But, you don't do that!** You don't even try to appeal to his sight anymore, by keeping your body in shape, dressing sexy, coming to bed sexy, yet you want us to compliment you on your sexiness, **WHAT SEXINESS?!!!!!** Yes, your ass looks fat in those jeans **LOSE SOME WEIGHT!!!!!** You think that sounds harsh but, you black women won't hesitate to tell us when we let ourselves go (Just let me hear you deny it!), but you want us to except you as is!!

Stroking his ego: The Responds He Lives For

Another thing you as black women don't do is you don't take the time to stroke a man's ego. A lot you black women (especially you so called *"Independent got it going on sistas"*) you won't take the time to make a man feel like a man. You're to busy trying to *"play it cool"* or you're just too proud as we said in **"The Pride Factor"** to give him praise. Keep in mind like we said in **"Why Black Men Crossover"** a man will gravitate toward the strongest praise and support! Just because you hold the title of *"wife"* or *"the woman that stuck with him through the bad times"* doesn't mean that you are excluded from this rule as well! See, I really have to get on these type of black women, because you think you are exempt from the rules of this chapter because *"you were there for him when nobody else was"*, but as you can see, men leave all the time for a white woman or an Asian woman, or some other race that's a gold digger who wants nothing but his money, but understands the basic principles of stimulating his sight(getting dolled up, working out, looking their absolute best,) stroking his ego(telling him how great he is, and how wonderful he's doing at his job, or being just as excited about an idea he has) and fulfilling his basic sexual urge(giving him the kind of sex he wants, when he wants it, for how long he wants it, no matter what, **NO EXCUSES!!!**)

An Example
by Jacquiez Douglas

Say there's a star college ball player, (we'll call him Tony) he's star athlete, has a great future ahead of him, and life looks very promising. Tony just played the biggest game of his life, he rushed for 395 yards and scored 4 touchdowns; he's on top of the world! Now after the game he's partying, feeling good about himself and naturally wants what every man wants after a major victory in life he wants some praise and victory ass! So, he steps to a sista with confidence, he's feeling good about himself, as he should! But, before he can even get his mouth open here she comes with her **"B.B.A."**, *"Oh, I'm supposed to be all up under you, because you rushed for 395 yards?"* *"I'm supposed to just bend over this couch, just because you scored 4 touchdowns?"* *"Nigga, you ain't all that!"* *"I ain't doing shit!!"* Blown away and flabbergasted, he backs off, but not before "Becky" the white girl comes to his rescue! She makes him feel like a man. **"OH-MY-GOD!!!!"** *"You were so freakin' awesome!"* *"I've never seen anybody move like that in my life!"* She dances with him, she's laughing with him, she's holding him, then eventually she tells him *"Let's go back to my place!!"* So now Tony's kicking it with the white girl and you're on the outskirts screaming **"SELLOUT!!"** All because you didn't follow the basic fundamental principles of catching, and maintaining a man. The saddest part of all this is "Becky" looks nowhere near as good as "Ki-Ki", but simply following the basic principles, and applying them, Becky now has an NFL player boyfriend living the good life, while you're stuck at home broke with a dead end 9-5, with your pride and sex toys hollering *"Men ain't shit!!!"* Now, tell me who just won in this scenario?

To The Black Women of America

In this final address, I will discuss the issues that plague each division of black women in America. Though the basic need isn't being meet, there's a specific attitude behind each group that I want to get at:

To The Opinionated Black Woman

The black woman that's always saying what's on her mind, and **"being real"** and **"telling it like it is"** as so many of you put it, I convict you. You shoot yourselves in the foot all the time, and sabotage your own relationship and/

or marriages with that big mouth of yours! You are unable to hold your peace, you say the first thing that comes to your head and it's killing your relationships! If he's acting a fool, sometimes the best reaction you can give is no reaction at all. Believe it or not that'll get him in line a lot quicker than you ranting and raving and running off at the mouth! Not everything that's thought needs to be said! Sometimes you gotta know when to hold your peace and let God deal with him, instead of always putting in your 2 cents! I know what you black women are saying right now: *"Well, I can't help it I just got to say something!"* **AND THAT'S YOUR PROBLEM NOW!!! YOU ALWAYS GOT TO SAY SOMETHING!!!!** The last thing a man wants to do, is feel like he's being confronted; it puts him in fight mode! Even if he's dealing with his woman or wife his defenses go up immediately and then it's no longer about communicating, but defending himself, his honor and setting you straight! Listen black women, there's a time when you can win **the argument, but lose the man!!!** And even though he may not have left you physically or divorced you, mentally, emotionally, and even spiritually he's abandoned you! Because you just had to **"get a word in edgewise"** you just lost your man! You're not strong, you're **FOOLISH**!! You're foolish and childish, to feel you always have to get the last word in. You're harming yourselves. Think about it.

To The Lazy Black Woman:

You **wicked** and **slothful** woman!! You lose your men/husbands and you damn well ought to!!! You are notorious for doing what it takes to get a man but, **won't** do what it takes to keep him! You are the women who say: **"I can't wait to get married, so I can just let myself go!"** What kind of trifling ignorance is that to say?! You women feel that since you caught the prize now *"I no longer have to put out, whenever he wants!" "I can gain 60 pounds and there's no problem with it, because he has to accept me as is!" "I don't have to do the all wild, crazy, and freaky things I used to do with, "Tom", "Dick", and "Harry", because I'm married now!" "I don't have to give him 45 minute blowjobs till he cries and blacks out anymore"* **THE DEVIL IS A LIE!!!!** This pretty much describes most of you black women in America! I convict you, for this lackadaisical, *"I don't have to try anymore"* attitude you seem to have about marriage and/or serious relationships! **Get this straight!** Marriage is not some retirement home for ex party girls, hookers, and ho's looking to hang up their thongs, party hats and good times!!! It is the most highest, most honored, and sacred form of relationship that God ever created! And shame on you for thinking so little of it, that you don't give it your all!

How much respect does that show for your husband to deny him the things that made you feel the most alive?! Keep in mind you have to spend the rest of your life with this man, you had better do your damnedest to keep him intrigued and excited about coming home. That's why a lot of black men don't come straight home, because honestly **there's nothing to come home to!!!** Come home to what? You dressed in your Grandma's bloomers?! That **lint infested rag** you call pajamas? Those thick ass tube socks, fuckin' rollers, and mud masks on your face? Then it's the same **boring ass** sex you had two days ago!! You did all kinds of wild and crazy shit when you ran with the other dudes, but now you can't bring yourself to do it with your husband or serious boyfriend? **You are selfish!! Plain and simple!!! No way around it!!!** You should be doing everything in your power to keep him happy, satisfied and desiring you!!! He's the only one who knew about your shady past and loved you anyway! He's the only one who knows how many men you've **REALLY** slept with and loves you anyway! He's the only one who's **patient** enough, while you went through your issues, problems and hard times! And finally, he's the only one who wanted to marry your tired, worn out, partied to death ass, because he still sees something special in you in spite of the **bullshit** you've now become!!

The Career Driven/Independent Black Woman

You by far are the worst of the bunch! I hope every career, independent, successful black woman reads and listens to this very carefully. And this includes you celebrity black women as well because this has become a spiritual issue with you all, so I'll have to be more frank and explicit with you! You career and independent women have become so high minded, so stubborn, so hateful and arrogant, that nobody can tell you anything! You all have become so **HELL BENT** on proving that you don't need a man, and you can get it yourself, that you've built a wall of standards and expectations that's virtually impossible for any man to climb **RICH** or **POOR!!!!** You are so proud and set in your ways that **NOTHING** and **NO ONE** is good enough for you!! You refuse to submit to anyone or anything. You think you can have it **all** in every single way, but here's a reality check: **NOBODY** can have it all!!! I know it's the cliché thing to say, *"You can have it all!!! Great illustrious careers, run* *your own fortune 500 company, raise the kids, be a wife and have the husband of your dreams!!!"* Now, all that sounds good on **paper**, but let's be real for a moment shall we?! The bottom line is marriage and/or a real relationship requires **SACRIFICE!!**

You got to give up something to get something else! You should have a basic understanding of that, because that's what got you where you are today. The problem is you don't wanna sacrifice anything in your career; you will always put your career first over your man or husband! Now I can't speak much for boyfriends, but let me tell you something to all to you married career women out there, and the one's looking to get married. Your husband and your marriage comes before any career you will ever have!! I don't give a damn what's going on in your career, your **first** priority is to please and make your husband happy!! **Everything else is on hold!** I can hear most of you black career women and celebrities saying it now, *"Oh, well, guess I ain't getting married then!!"* or *"Guess I won't have a husband for too much longer!"* And that's sad. Doesn't surprise me one bit but still sad nonetheless. Your high mindedness has gotten so bad, you feel you don't need anyone or anything, including men period! Many independent women are screwing other women not out of sexual preference, but out of just sheer **arrogance!** They've gotten so **"independent"** so **"self sufficient"** That you've completely written men out of your life period! You're so out to prove that you don't want a man, don't need a man, ain't thinking bout a man, that you've completely crossed over to the "other side" just to **"prove a point!!"** Since you all are now coming into power just like us now it's my duty to tell you you're gonna eventually become us. *"Can't no man tell me shit"* is what you say. *"I'm just as powerful and equal to a man"* you say. Yeah, you're right. You're just as powerful, just as equal, and you're gonna be just as **LONLEY**, just as **MISERABLE**, and you're gonna be just as **DEAD** as well!!!!! And, ultimately you're gonna be just as **JUDGED**, because **pride cometh before the fall!!** You just can't bring your self to submit to man because that would be too much like admitting "defeat" in your eyes. So you devote your entire life to some false ideology that *"you don't need him"* and you die alone!

The Christian Black Woman

Last, but certainly not least, I address you Christian black women; while you're not as lazy, or arrogant, or even opinionated like your sisters, your case is still the most severe. Seeing that Christians are the highest among the divorce rate, I must convict you as well. I wouldn't call Christian black woman evil, arrogant or lazy, but you're extremely naïve and disillusioned. There's an old saying that goes *"You've become so spiritually minded, that you're no earthly good"* You women tend **over spiritualize** everything in your life, including your sex life and romantic life as well! When your husband wants to do something wild and freaky, you're quick to hide behind scriptures and holy dancing as opposed to dealing with reality. You're so busy trying to be **"deep"** and **"holy"** that your marriage is in shambles and you're gonna be holy dancing your ass to divorce court just like the rest of the world!

Christian women, I love you, but you tend to sometimes not live in reality. You have to realize that a man saved or unsaved has the same basic needs and principles to feeling like a man, and also has the same urges. You think because he's saved he's protected from temptation but he's not! The truth is he's probably tempted more because of his conviction to do the right thing makes him more of a target for the enemy! If he stopped working and didn't pay the bills, and you confronted him about it and he started speaking in tongues (ee-ma-ma, ee-ma-ma) you'd have a problem with that wouldn't you?! But, you say *"Well, that's "reality", if he don't pay the bills we're gonna be homeless!"* Well, here's some **"reality"** for you, if you don't submit yourself to his wants, needs and desires you're gonna be **"replaced"! Stop hiding behind the bible!** That's what's getting you in trouble now! You go to church to escape real life and real situations, and then you use the bible and scriptures to inflict guilt on your man or husbands for feeling something that's totally God given and you're **losing the men!!!**

Conclusion

As you can see we've pretty much covered the entire spectrum of why black women are alone or can't keep a man. We covered their many problems in chapter 1; we've discussed their conditional love giving in "The If Factor", their constant need to be mistreated and abused in "The Masochistic Mind" Their sneaky ass tactics in the "Friend Factor", their out right selfish **me, me, me** attitude, their **foolish, foolish** pride in the "The Pride Factor" and finally why black men **REALLY** do crossover! We know we will receive a lot of persecution for writing this book, from black women, and **black men** that say they agree with the black women, and that they hate it as well. But we can assure you the only reason they're saying that is because they don't want to be called **"sexist"** and **"chauvinistic"** They're also afraid that they won't get **laid** any more! That's why a lot of men back down from these women! Women give them that look or they blurt out loud **EXCUSE ME?!!!** Anytime a man tries to go against her, or make a comment stating his male beliefs!

We've all been seeing it since we were kids. All those sitcoms we saw where the woman raised up against the man and he cowered down to the woman. Especially in a lot of black sitcoms!! **What are you afraid of black men?!!** That she won't **"put out"** any more? If she doesn't then get rid of her **immediately!!** If she's **that** petty **(like most black women are)** to not give you some because you made a statement that you believe in or stand by, then she wasn't worth shit to begin with! (Bullard) "This is largely in part, because most men aren't as Tariq "K-Flex" Nasheed said in his book "The Art of Mackin", **"Sexually disciplined"** and most men can't control their sexual appetite, and feel they **"got to have it all the time!!"**. This is a weakness that most women know **(All women!)** and use that weakness against them." And here's a little tip for you fellas, if you keep cowering down to her when she does that, that'll just give more and more power! She'll think she can control you with her **"coochie"** and will always threaten to take it away from you if you get out of line. Kick that bitch to the curve!! Tell her *"fuck you, and your "coochie" bitch!!"*, and just walk away. We guarantee she'll come around sooner than you think, and if she doesn't then **"to hell with her!!!"**

Before you crucify the two of us, please keep in mind that we we're not talking about all black women, like we said in the intro of this book, just **SOME** of you! And please take notice to the one's that are furious at this book and are steaming right now, are you mad because you are offended? Or are you mad because somewhere in these chapters you found yourself, and you're subconscious (or God, whatever you want to call it!) there's a little voice that's telling you *"they're right!"*

There are some really good black women out there, black women who handle their business and take care of their men. There are also some "mature" black women that will read this and apply it to their lives and actually sit there and think *"maybe, if I at least **try** these things they said then maybe I might actually be able to get a man (and keep him!)"* A lot of black women say *"Well, I do all these things that these "so-called" other races you say do but my man/husband still treats me like crap so what you got to say about that?"* Well, unfortunately there are some men in this world that are going to mistreat you no matter how good you are to them. In that case you should just leave him alone and move on to somebody who really appreciates you. There are some black women who will play the "insecurity card" on us to make themselves feel better. Let us give you a brief rundown of what just some those excuses will be:

1.) *"They're just a bunch of insecure men, who are looking for women to control and dominate!"*

2.) *"They're just a bunch of lames that could never get women, and now they're just lashing out!"*

3.) *"They're a bunch of bitter, angry black men, who didn't have enough game to hang with black women!"*

4.) *"They just have small penises and now they're mad at the world and everyone in it!"*

What ever they have to say to themselves to keep from admitting the truth, that the problem is **them!** Let us ask you this, black women. Even if we are **bitter** and **angry** as I'm sure you have said about a thousand times while you were reading this book, does that make anything we said in this book less true?! (Bullard) **"Think about it!"**

We can assure you that these excuses couldn't be further from the truth. We've all had our fair share of women, it's just that we were getting tired of giving and getting less back than what we gave, or getting nothing at all! Between the two of us we finally realized that it **"Just ain't worth the hassle!"** and we'd be much happier pursuing other options. We also know that a lot of black women will automatically compare themselves to white women as far as to what we said about their problems and issues. They'll say: *"I know white women, Asian women, and Latino women who do the exact same thing we do!!"* And like we said in the beginning of this book, we're not referring to **all of them**, like we're not referring all of you! But, you gotta admit, they don't have nearly **HALF** the problems you black women have keeping their men!!! (Bullard) *"And, **stop worrying about them, and focus on yourself!!** You're the one's that are statistically the least desirable of all races of women!!!"* To our good black women out there, and to the **"mature"** one's who are going to use this and apply it to make themselves better, we got love for you all because you finally got the gist of this book! Use it as constructive criticism and apply it to your situation. Black men as we said earlier, let this along with the Holy Bible be your guide to find the right woman for you, and don't be afraid to challenge them on these subject matters we talked about. We know a lot of people will not feel this book, or like it because they say it's *"too crass"* or *"we're not doctors or any type of specialists in relationships, so we can't possibly know what were talking about"*, but we don't have to be any of that to know what's going on in the streets and every day life. It's easy to see what is in plain view, if you just truly open your eyes and don't just look, but **pay attention!** Don't just hear, but **listen** to what black men are saying, what they're doing, what they're **not** saying, what they're **not** doing!!

Most men, when they stop talking that's a bigger cause to be worried than when he's going off! Because one of two things are about to happen; either he's about to whoop your ass, or he's completely checked out emotionally, mentally, even sometimes spiritually from you and he's two steps from leaving. So black women, please get yourselves together. We're not trying to blast you just for the hell of it! We're just trying to open your eyes, and make you see what you're doing to the good black men. That's right we said **GOOD** black men, this book isn't for you **trifling ass, abusive, no good** men either! Men who stay all up at their woman's house eating up all the food, not contributing in any way but sexually! We hope you were not screaming and shouting at this book either, because this sure as **hell** isn't for you!

Most of you black women we mentioned in this book, are not bad or evil people, you just have twisted ways of thinking and logic. We love you, you may not believe that but we do! And we believe that some of you have the possibility to be some of the greatest women/wives that God ever created. We really do believe that, but you gotta get yourselves together!! You better get your priorities in order and get your issues straight. The Bible says to *"Speak the truth in love"* and that's what we're doing and that's what we'll continue to do until the day we die!

<u>Final Quotes</u>

Jaquiez: "The views and comments expressed in this book are derived from my own personal experiences with black and white women. I've had my own personal share of good and bad experiences with black and white women. Unfortunately the majority of the bad experiences have come from black women. Black women have a tendency to be more prudish and bitchy than white or any other race of women for that matter. I only speak through this book; because of my different experiences and things I see everyday. I'm a good man and I know it, and black women have always taken advantage of that, and used it for there own benefit. The only woman that ever treated me worth while was a white woman, or other women out side of my own race. Please don't be under the misconception that I hate black women and that I'm speaking negatively of all black women, because I'm not. There are some black women in this world, that are great women,(and I have known & dated some) who handle their business and take care of there man, and for that I tip my hat to you.

But, there are more than a few bad apples that make even the good ones look bad. That is who I'm speaking of, and they know who they are! If I said any thing to offend anyone … screw it, I don't care. It's about time that this matter be brought to light, after being taboo and kept in the dark for so long! Black women claim that they're "Nubian Queens", but after you get to know them, and then you find out that they're no more than "Nubian Nuisances!" If you want to call your self a queen, you should conduct yourself as such, with class and humility. We are making these views known in hopes that black women will take notice to what they already know and make an attempt to better themselves. If they don't, that's fine too, sad but fine! Just don't continue to ask yourself the question as to why you're still **alone** or can't keep a man!

What I like

The type of woman I'm looking for first and foremost is beautiful in mind, body and spirit. Nice body, in shape, likes to keep herself up for her man. She likes to dress sexy on a regular basis. Since I love a lot of different women I'd like her be bi-sexual and have a high sex drive. Drama free, knows how to be submissive and dominant, when it's time to be dominant. Body wise, I like a woman that has a great lower torso, nice legs, a great ass, and beautiful feet. A sexual free spirit, someone who knows how to keep my attention, and will try anything twice. She has no mentality of the words "woulda, coulda, shoulda"! A woman that's happy being a loving housewife, she's willing to do anything with me. She has to love to pamper her man, and appreciate being pampered by me. As far as her race goes it's a very slim chance that you will find a black woman with all these traits. **That's why I prefer a white woman!"**

Hank: "I came up with the concept to write this book because for many years I have seen too many black women lie, manipulate, and scheme their way to get too many things. I also had the unfortunate displeasure of being the victim of some of these black women's schemes. I admit it, I've played the fool before (As the song goes!), but maybe that's because I was raised to always give people the benefit of the doubt, **LOL**, A lot of good that did!!! But, I don't trip over it, everything happens for a reason as they say. Of all the different jobs I have had, it's given me the opportunity to talk to different women both black and white. And I've also gotten the chance to talk to other black men and get their perspective of things as well. And something that myself, and Jaquiez came to realize is that we're not the only ones that feel this way! We're not the only one's that are frustrated and tired of the attitude and problems, and worse the fact, that you know you have a problem and **won't** do anything about it!

As Jaquiez said in his quote most of you black women know you have a problem, but yet do nothing to solve it. I can't tell you how sad and heartbreaking that is! To have an issue that can be solved with just a few minor adjustments, but still choose not to do it. Unlike my partner Jaquiez I'm still on the fence about the whole swearing off black women thing. I have seen some of the most amazing spiritual and mental connections between black men and black women, connections I've never seen anywhere else with any other race of people. And while I questioned the men they did it for, I couldn't help but be moved by the commitment and perseverance they showed by sticking by their man/or husband. In my personal opinion, **there's nothing stronger, more powerful, or more beautiful than the love of a black woman.** I just wish they would do it for the right man that's all.

I've experienced this love for myself; the woman I mentioned in the "Friend Factor" was one of them. Most people aren't blessed to find something like that in their lifetime, that's why it was so difficult to let her go like that. That's why I know it will be difficult for a lot of guys that feel that way about certain women in their life, to just let them go. It will be hard but trust me it's a necessity! It's not like I **wanted** to cut her out of my life, but when you're giving more than you're getting, it will literally **drain you!** And I don't want to see that happen to my **good** brothers out there. You're worth more than that!"

What I like

"The kind of woman I like physical wise: I like tall women, with **big breasts!** Though I'm not against short women either, just as long as you've got **big breasts!** (The physical is not as important as what's on the inside though.) Long hair, thick thighs, and sexy feet. A woman who keeps herself maintained at all times (manicure, pedicure, getting hair done) likes to work out and is **not lazy!** Personality wise: **I LOVE BI-SEXUAL WOMEN!!!!!** She's really into other women and not afraid to walk up to one and ask her if she wants to come home with us. That's right! I love a **bold, aggressive, kinky** woman that's not afraid to see something she wants and go right after it! Someone that's not shy about her sexuality and fetishes, someone who's got my back no matter what! Spiritual wise: She has to be a giving person, someone who treats people the way, she wants to be treated! Someone with a spirit so amazing that, she can calm me down by just walking into the room. Her entire presence is just soothing. It doesn't matter what color she is, because frankly I don't care. I don't' think all black women are hopeless so I'm not as quick to write you off yet."

"I just hope that I can change at least one person male or female by this book. And, I sincerely hope someone finds their way and gets their life back on track. Thank you for reading our book. God bless you and God keep you.... And, remember gentlemen **IT JUST AIN'T WORTH THE HASSLE!!!!**"

Author Bios

Jaquiez (pronounced Ja-qwez) Douglas was born Oct. 9, 1979 in Dallas Texas but was raised in Memphis, Tennessee most of his life. An ex- football player, Jaquiez and Hank met at an Ole Miss football camp their senior year of high school and have been best friends ever since. Having dated many women in and out of his race, Jaquiez considers himself quite knowledgeable in the art of dating and was eager to contribute to this project.

Henry E. Bullard, III or "Hank" as most people call was born November 22, 1978 in San Diego, California. A "Navy Brat" Hank has lived in Virginia Beach, Virginia, Seattle, Washington, and Memphis, Tennessee where he currently resides. Hank was always fascinated as to the "Why" in human behavior which is why psychology was always his favorite subject. Hank was inspired to write "Why Black Women Are Alone" After so many females would ask him why they can't keep a man or why they always pick the wrong man, and is the narrator throughout most of the book. Hank is also a poet with a book due out next year.